A HANDBOOK OF ASEAN BUSINESS CASES:
EMERGING ISSUES IN BUSINESS AND MANAGEMENT

MAIZAITULAIDAWATI MD HUSIN
HALIYANA KHALID
SHATHEES BASKARAN
NOMAHAZA MAHADI

PARTRIDGE

Copyright © 2021 by Husin, Khalid, Baskaran, Mahadi.

ISBN:	Softcover	978-1-5437-6703-2
	eBook	978-1-5437-6704-9

All rights reserved. No part of this book may be used or reproduced by any means, graphic, electronic, or mechanical, including photocopying, recording, taping or by any information storage retrieval system without the written permission of the author except in the case of brief quotations embodied in critical articles and reviews.

Because of the dynamic nature of the Internet, any web addresses or links contained in this book may have changed since publication and may no longer be valid. The views expressed in this work are solely those of the author and do not necessarily reflect the views of the publisher, and the publisher hereby disclaims any responsibility for them.

Print information available on the last page.

To order additional copies of this book, contact
Toll Free +65 3165 7531 (Singapore)
Toll Free +60 3 3099 4412 (Malaysia)
orders.singapore@partridgepublishing.com

www.partridgepublishing.com/singapore

CONTENTS

About the Authors vii

Case # 1 What Matters Most To The Implementation of Management Information System: Human or System Factors? ...1

Case # 2 Online Fraud is Now Rife: The Case of Mercu Suria Bank Berhad 12

Case # 3 3T's of Start-Up from Scratch: Task, Tools, and Techniques 19

Case # 4 Don't Be A Copycat, Designers! 43

Case # 5 Ayub Seafood Bangi: Which Way To Go? 56

Case # 6 Street Food Concept: A Case Study On Mekcha Kopitiam 84

Case # 7 Nextra: Inefficiency in Managing Cleaning Service Contractor 111

ABOUT THE AUTHORS

Adriana Mohd Rizal (PhD) is a Senior Lecturer at Azman Hashim International Business School, Universiti Teknologi Malaysia. She obtained her BBA from the University of Wisconsin Milwaukee, USA, her Executive MBA from University Teknologi MARA, and her Doctorate of Business Administration from UKM-GSB, Universiti Kebangsaan Malaysia. Her research interests include entrepreneurship and innovation, social entrepreneurship, and SME new creation and development.

David Ling Kim Hui holds an MBA from Universiti Teknologi Malaysia and a Bachelor's degree in Engineering majoring in Electronics Telecommunications from Malaysia Multimedia University. He is a seasoned Supply Manager who has a strong passion for material management and related areas.

Ebtihal Ebrahim is a Product Manager at Hadath App, having completed her MBA in Healthcare Management in Azman Hashim International Business School. She has more than 15 years of experience in designing digital products and managing digital marketing. She is active in consultancy projects for government institutions and entrepreneurs in Riyadh.

Haliyana Khalid (PhD, CPM (Asia)) is a senior lecturer at Azman Hashim International Business School, UTM. She obtained her PhD in Computing, with specialization in Human Computer Interaction from Lancaster University, UK. She holds a professional certificate in marketing. Haliyana research interests are in the horizon of information systems and digital marketing.

Maizaitulaidawati Md Husin (PhD) is an experienced academician with strong enthusiasm and passion for Islamic banking and finance. She is currently an associate professor at Azman Hashim International Business School, Universiti Teknologi Malaysia and an adjunct research fellow at University of Business and Technology, Jeddah, Saudi Arabia. She has over 12 years of experience in teaching and supervision. Mai holds a PhD in Islamic Economics, MSc in Banking, and BBA in Finance. Visit her professional website at http://www.maizaitulaidawati.com/.

Naharudin Saadan, C.A(M) is an accountant in the Accountant General Department of Malaysia. He holds a bachelor's in accountancy from Universiti Utara Malaysia and MBA from Universiti Teknologi Malaysia. He has served in various federal and state government agencies in Malaysia and has vast experience in public sector financial management.

Nomahaza Mahadi (PhD) is an Associate Professor at Azman Hashim International Business School, UTM. She graduated from the University of Southampton UK with her PhD degree. She has more than ten years of experience in the area of emotional intelligence, personality, leadership and work attitudes.

Nor Aiza Mohd Zamil (PhD) is a senior lecturer of Accounting at International Business School, Universiti Teknologi Malaysia. Upon completion of her first degree (Bachelor of Accounting

(Hons.)) from International Islamic University Malaysia (IIUM), she started his career as a finance executive at Multimedia Development Corporation. Then she continued to pursue her study in MSc in Accounting at IIUM. She has received her PhD from Cardiff Business School, United Kingdom. Her main research interest includes Islamic banking and finance, Islamic Accounting, banking efficiency and Shari'ah Governance in Islamic financial institutions.

Ong Choon Hee (PhD) is a senior lecturer at Azman Hashim International Business School, Universiti Teknologi Malaysia. He received his Doctorate in Business Administration from Universiti Utara Malaysia. His areas of research interest are organizational behavior, talent management and technology management.

Sare Yasseen Iderosee is currently an active wealth planner agent with Prudential Assurance Malaysia Berhad, passionate in sales and helping people with planning their wealth and financial objectives. Previously she served one of the retail companies in Malaysia. She received her first-degree education from Universiti Putra Malaysia (UPM) in Bachelor Science (Human Development & Information Technology) and continue to pursue her Master's Degree in Business Administration at Universiti Teknologi Malaysia (UTM).

Shathees Baskaran (PhD) has a Bachelor of Economics from Universiti Putra Malaysia, an MBA (Accountancy), and a Doctor of Business Administration from Universiti Utara Malaysia. He is a faculty member at Azman Hashim International Business School, Universiti Teknologi Malaysia. His areas of interest are strategic management, entrepreneurship, and related behavioral studies.

Siti Zaleha Abdul Rasid (PhD) is an associate professor in management accounting at Azman Hashim International Business School, Universiti Teknologi Malaysia. She has a PhD in accounting from the International Islamic University, Malaysia. She is also an associate member of the Malaysian Institute of Accountant, and her research interests are in management accounting, risk management and corporate governance.

Supamah Krishnan is an accounting lecturer at a private college. She received her Master of Business Administration from Universiti Teknologi Malaysia. Her areas of research interest are organizational behavior and organizational development.

Suzilawati Kamarudin (PhD) is from Universiti Teknologi Malaysia and currently is seconded to the University of Business and Technology Jeddah, Kingdom of Saudi Arabia. Her research focus is on small and medium enterprises and marketing. Her research grant amounted to more than 1.5 million. Her works have been published in reputable journals, book chapters and cases.

Theresa Ho Char Fei (PhD) is a senior lecturer at Azman Hashim International Business School, UTM. She teaches strategic management and management-related subjects. Theresa has published her research works in indexed international journals, including the Journal of Asia Pacific Business, Global Business Review and Journal of Relationship Marketing. Her research interests are in the areas of Entrepreneurship and Intellectual Capital.

CASE #1

What Matters Most To The Implementation of Management Information System: Human or System Factors?

Ong Choon Hee, Supamah Krishnan, Maizaitulaidawati Md Husin and Adriana Mohd Rizal

The problem begins

In July 2018, Sally, the CFO of Dinar Medical Devices (DMD), discussed with Jacob, The CEO of DMD and Johnson, the Head of the Information System of DMD, and other heads of departments about the issues faced by the finance department. The meeting was arranged due to the problems that emerged between the finance, information system, and other related departments. In this meeting, Sally, the CFO of DMD, explained the issues they faced during the month-end processing and errors in the MIS BT IV system while posting reports. She expressed that, due to these problems, the finance team had to work extra hours to correct the errors manually. This situation incurred overtime costs and additional workload for them. Furthermore, due to this unexpected problem, they suffered from currency exchange rates difference where DMD could not collect payment from its affiliates. This situation resulted in a shortage of collections during the month-end of the accounts closing period.

Due to the delay in report submission, DMD receives complaints from the Head Quarter located in Singapore. In the meeting, Jacob and Johnson propose some measures to the finance team to help solve the staff's issues in the finance department. Both Jacob and Johnson suggest sending the finance team for additional courses to get some extra information and knowledge about the systems and errors that occurred during month-end processing. However, Sally disagrees with this suggestion as the majority of the finance staff were seniors. Some have worked for DMD for more than 10 years and attended all the existing system's training modules. Moreover, they are the experts on the BT IV system. Sally insisted that DMD uses the old version of BT IV, where the rest of the affiliates were using the up-to-date versions. Upgrading the old system is necessary for DMD finance staff to convert their report into the required formats and submit it to the head-quarter and related affiliates for month-end closing. In the opinion of Sally, upgrading the old version system is the only way to overcome the problems and other related issues.

Besides, the new version can help the finance team complete their reports on time instead of having to work overtime where it was too stressful for them. Johnson agrees with Sally's suggestion, but he does not support the idea of an immediate upgrade of the existing system. He opined that without proper investigation and identification of the root causes, upgrading the current system may eventually lead to a similar situation. Instead, Johnson proposes a thorough investigation of the issues that happened mainly during the month-end closing. According to Johnson's understanding, the existing BT IV system is compatible with the other reporting systems that the head-quarter and affiliates are using. Therefore, he would like to challenge the finance team to seek a practical solution rather than jumping to a conclusion without identifying the root causes.

Jacob urged Sally to follow Johnson's advice without any delay to find the actual causes of the issues that could affect DMD's performance. His concerns were more on the human factors than the system factors. Sally immediately excused herself from the meeting and made a phone call to the finance manager to arrange a meeting on the same date at 5.30 pm. Later, Sally discussed with the finance team and explained the instructions from the top management. The finance team understands the current situation, and they give full cooperation in investigating the issues. Subsequently, they form a task-force committee to investigate the issues that hinder month-end reports processing and posting. A task-force committee headed by Janice, a senior finance manager, and other accounts payable and receivable team members begin their tasks immediately the next day to get to the bottom of the issues. They were given two weeks to investigate the situation and then present the outcomes to the top management. The top management expects to get the issues resolved before the next month-end closing begins. The task-force team was told to discuss with other departments and work with them to identify any possible reasons that may cause the delay in posting the reports to the BT IV system.

After 2 weeks, the investigation was over, and all are expected to report to the chief financial officer. Sally has been following up with the finance staff on the process of investigation since the first day. During the 2 weeks, Sally noticed how the finance team works and how effective their communication and relationship among the co-workers. She has further convinced herself that most finance staff work until late at night to complete their tasks, and some even skip their lunch break and do their job. However, they did not discover any mal-practices or misalignment of the procedures caused by human factors. This has given Sally great confidence to present their findings to the top management and confirmed that the system solely caused the problems. Sally waits for the finance staff's final report and expects their findings to be more reasonable and valid. Sally can't wait to present the investigation outcomes to top management to upgrade the BT IV system immediately. However, things did not go the way they wish.

Dinar Medical Devices: An overview

Dinar Medical Devices (DMD) has been established in 1987. DMD is one of the major manufacturers of digital hearing instruments, utilized modern microelectronic technology. DMD has remained a leader in the hearing aid industry, developed many innovative products or goods. The innovative products are the pocket size hearing instrument, remote control for hearing technology, trainable hearing instrument, and other digital hearing aids. DMD recognized Asia-Pacific at an early stage as a key market. By 1997 the company was represented throughout the region with 5,000 employees, around 5 joint ventures and over 10 plants. Since the end of the 1990s, DMD has been focusing even more on optimizing its business portfolio through divestments, acquisitions, the formation of new companies, and the founding of joint ventures.

DMD is one of the responsible employers, which recognizes its activities impact the society in which it operates. DMD understands that an important element of corporate social responsibility is how their activities affect their customers, employees, business partners, shareholders, public entities, and society in various ways and how they meet their obligations to all those stakeholders. In addition, DMD is one of the organizations operating in several markets and industries with a specific product and service portfolio. Operating on such a large scale brings a high level of responsibility, which DMD takes extremely seriously. For DMD, corporate responsibility means that they safeguard the success and future of their company by taking into account economic, social, ethical and environmental concerns.

As an active supporter of the local community and environment, DMD encourages its employees to get involved in volunteering programs supports the community through charity fundraising, partners with educational establishment to support business educational programs, support local environmental charities with volunteering and sponsorship, compliance and corporate governance forms the basis of all their decision making and monitoring processes. DMD's strengths are mainly on a wider range of services offerings, the latest innovation in their products, ideas, solutions, leading competitive position and strong brand name. All DMD employees are directed and motivated towards one goal. DMD produces products that customers use in their daily life, and their production lines fit the use of many customers in our society. DMD is very creative and innovative in production as it constantly updates its products and looks for new solutions to develop the products.

The finance department: A system failure or a fiasco

Janice led the finance department in DMD with a team of accounting staff to manage accounts tasks such as accounts payable, intercompany clearance process, high risks payments, fixed assets, major export services, tax calculation and financial statements. With a team of 7 members, including Janice, they are handling all the ongoing financial tasks for the company. Janice instructed all the person-in-charge for each area to investigate and list errors and difficulties when they report their works into the system. For instance, the accounts payable officer feedback that the purchase approval process was not supported by BT IV effectively where there was a huge number of invoices and price variances. All the payment invoices have to be processed one by one, and the batch process was not allowed. After keying the information into the system, the officer still needs to check the list display by the system against the actual invoices. The matter becomes worse when she has to manually contact the suppliers or creditors once the payment is released. The current system did not prompt the receivers, thus requiring the officer to do extra work due to the system's inefficiency. Further, the system was not able to supply information to the banks to release payments. Hence, manual work is required to ensure the payments were not rejected automatically when no details are provided. Most of the time, the officer has to work until late at night to overcome these issues where it makes her exhausted, and sometimes the intention to leave the company crosses her mind.

As for intercompany clearance activities, the finance staff always faced issues in collecting invoices from the affiliates. Due to the delay in obtaining invoices, the system rejects the posted invoices, and extra work must be carried out manually. The system does not provide flexibility for the staff to handle the issue due to unforeseen circumstances, mal-practices or human errors. The officer did highlight an important point that the finance department will be blamed for the inability to perform intercompany clearance activities on time. However, the actual scenario is caused by the sensitivity and inflexibility of the system. She felt helpless in this situation. On the other hand, the BT IV system does not help much in high-risk handling payment. Normally, payments were not arranged earlier but had to delay until the due date is approaching. This is because the BT IV system does not allow high-risk payment to proceed without approval from the top management, and there are no other alternatives to get it done. It sometimes took a long time for the management to approve, which has dragged the process to the due date.

Besides, fixed assets have also become an issue in BT IV. The fixed asset calculation was incorrect in the system. The system could not calculate the depreciation values based on the book values in a fixed percentage. In particular, the depreciation values, repair costs and other expenses were not allowed to be categorized as expenses in the system. Therefore, the officer-in-charge again has to adjust the values accordingly manually. If the values were not offset accordingly, the total value of assets would increase, becoming a serious issue at the end of the year. Eventually, it has reached a situation where the finance department even requested the company to purchase a separate fixed asset software to replace BT IV. However, the request was turned down by the management. Furthermore, the major export services report was also not supported by BT IV as the system does not have a function to import a document to update the information. This has resulted in insufficient information, and no updates can be done in real-time. Hence, whenever there is a request to look for recent updates in the system, they still have to refer to the list in an excel sheet. In short, the BT IV system did not support updating the major export services database at all.

Tax calculation is another issue that bothers the finance department. The BT IV was found not able to support the way the company prepares its tax calculation. This has led to an outcome where the records were not maintained efficiently. The staff feel that the system should be upgraded to suit the practices of the department. On top of that, financial statements like wages, EPF and tax do seem not totally with the manual records. Therefore, extra efforts have to be put forward to link manual records and online records together. This has further raised whether the staff is not competent or the system is not suitable for their works. To make matters worse, the finance staff were not authorized to change the settings in the system. Consequently, the staff were getting more frustrated as they have put in a lot of hard work, yet they got all the blame from other departments and the top management for not completing their tasks on time.

Shortage of manpower

Recently, the finance team was facing a shortage of manpower. There is no replacement for the two staff who had resigned some time ago. The management suggests the finance Manager maintain the current headcount and distribute the workload among the existing staff. In this case, the extra work that they received will create more pressure on them. This unexpected situation has caused some staff to be absent from work or take emergency leaves to excuse themselves from work. Nonetheless, the finance team did not maintain a good relationship with the other departments. This is because additional tasks make them work extra time until they have to skip their lunch breaks. In addition, most of them have a family and kids who need to be taken care of. Owing to this workload, the staff are lacking family time for their loved ones. This affects their emotions directly. When employees do not have a work-life balance, this causes more human errors at work.

No increment

The other issue highlighted by the finance staff was that, when the workload increase, their salaries and remuneration packages are still unchanged. There is no increment for them. This situation has caused disappointment among the staff. They feel that the management tends to ignore their concerns. As a result, the works they perform are not equitable to the rewards they receive.

Changes in the human resource department

Recently, there was a major change in the Human Resource department. The new human resource manager, Joanne and the recruitment staff were unable to manage the turnover issue in the finance department. They took a long time in searching for a replacement. The issue of manpower replacement is persisting in the middle of these problems, and further, aggravate the impacts on the finance department.

Job satisfaction level

The level of job satisfaction was found to be low among the finance department staff. Janice did highlight this issue to Sally, and she felt that this is unusual because all this while the staff were cooperative, capable and sincere. A majority of the staff have worked for more than 10 years in the company. It was highly unlikely that they wanted to leave the company because of a better offer elsewhere. The recent extra pressure on them may be the cause that triggers their unhappiness with the company. Some of the staff have started to ignore other departments' requests seeking help to solve issues related to accounts. The finance staff have become more defensive. As Janice mentioned: "There must be a reason behind all these, and I believe the system is the culprit."

Meeting with the management

The day to meet with the top management has come. All the related personnel was invited to the meeting room. Jacob, Johnson, Sally, Janice and the new human resource manager Joanne were in the meeting room. Jacob chaired the meeting by asking Sally to report the findings of the investigation. Sally acknowledged that the finance department has managed to identify various causes that caused the month-end closing issues. Besides, Sally added that there were major system errors and some human errors in this regard. However, these errors were not generated solely by the finance department but also by the other departments. Sally suggested that the management upgrade the system because it is linked with the other affiliates' databases. Besides, the system also has many restrictions when processing the data. Sally's presentation has raised the eyebrows of Jacob and Johnson as both of them do not agree with her. "What if we fail again after we've upgraded the system?" asked Jacob as he eyed the rest of them suspiciously.

Case questions

1. Diagnose the problems faced by DMD and explain how they affect the company performance?
2. Identify human and system factors that cause the problems?
3. If you were the CEO of DMD, what would you advise Sally to solve the problems in the finance department?
4. If you were Sally, what are the interventions that you will use to improve the performance of the finance department?

CASE #2

Online Fraud is Now Rife: The Case of Mercu Suria Bank Berhad

Maizaitulaidawati Md Husin, Ong Choon Hee and Adriana Mohd Rizal

Getting frustrated

"Although fraud is impossible to prevent fully, we can reduce the probability of fraud occurrence and minimize losses with stronger oversight and tighter controls," said Datuk Syarifah Ardaniah, one of the board of directors of Mercu Suria Bank Berhad to Aisha Riana. "As the chief information security manager of this company, I want you to find ways to overcome this issue. I want to see a fewer number of internet banking incidents in our next meeting. Otherwise, I might need to replace you with someone else more competent to do so." She continued. Aisha Riana still remembered the warning Datuk Syarifah Ardaniah to her in the committee meeting held in June, precisely six months ago. Aisha Riana was shocked. He could not believe what she just heard. "How could Datuk Syarifah Ardaniah do this to me," she murmured. "Do you have anything else to say?" said Datuk Syarifah Ardaniah to Aisha

Riana. "No, boss. I hope I will be able to investigate this issue and take preventive actions," said Aisha Riana before she leaves.

On the evening of 15 January 2021, Aisha Riana is still in the office, even though her working hours ended a few hours ago. "You are still here? Why don't you go back?" said Rahman, Aisha Riana's colleague. "I am nervous about attending the meeting tomorrow", Aisha Riana replied. "Number of the incident's become higher, and I am afraid Datuk Syarifah Ardaniah will be mad and fire me," she continued. "You have done your best, Aisha. So do not worry, and you'll be fine" Rahman tried to calm her down.

Mercu Suria Bank Berhad: An overview

Mercu Suria Bank Berhad (MSBB) has been established in 1967, a year after Malaysia gained its independence. After 30 years of establishment, MSBB has known as one of the country's largest financial services groups with an established presence in the ASEAN region. The bank also presents in other international financial centres like London, Beijing, New York, Frankfurt, and Hong Kong.

MSBB provides a full suite of conventional and Shariah-compliant products and services in commercial banking, investment banking, and insurance. MSBB was also known as Malaysia's nine Islamic banking players committed as an early adopter of Bank Negara Malaysia's Value-based Intermediation initiative. The initiative aimed to move the Islamic financial industry to the next level of growth by strengthening Islamic banking institutions' impact in generating positive and sustainable effects on the economy, environment, and society by relying on Shariah to determine underlying values and moral compass and priorities.

MSBB was outperformed in the industry and shine over the competitors. The bank has achieved several outstanding awards. In 2018, the bank received the Islamic Business and Finance Southeast Asia Award (IBFSA) 2018, Malaysia e-Payments Excellence Awards (MEEA) 2017, Best Equity House, Best Private Bank Malaysia Editors Award (PBMEA) and many other relevant awards at the local and international arena. MSBB also has outstanding contributions to the social welfare of the community. The bank has been awarded Prime Minister's corporate social responsibility awards in five consecutive years, from 2014 until 2019.

MSBB also surpassed industry performance on all fronts. As of 2019, the company has recorded a solid financial performance at RM2.3 million, which rose 5.1percent from a year before. In addition to that, The Bank's financing grew RM8.6 billion to reach RM80.9 billion in the same financial year, with asset quality remained strong and resilient, despite the robust expansion and challenging economic environment.

Online fraud

Online fraud and scams operate under different disguises and can be differentiated by many names, including consumer cybercrime, internet fraud, online crime, and e-crime. However, no matter what it is called, online fraud schemes steal millions of dollars each year from victims worldwide, and it causes considerable distress to everyone it affects. It can even culminate in serious financial problems, as some victims have discovered.

Online fraud was done via plaguing the internet through various methods such as data breaches, ransomware, phishing, and spoofing. Based on a statistic, more than one-third of cybersecurity events start with a phishing email or some malicious attachment in an email sent to personal emails and the corporate emails and employees of a company.

The "Macau Scam"

The "Macau scam" is believed to be originated from Macau and had operated from other countries such as Cambodia, Indonesia, the Philippines, and Thailand, therefore significantly reducing the risk of being detected and prosecuted. The scammers generally employed the same modus operandi, phoning victims while posing as bank officers or authorities using the Voice Over Internet Protocol (VOIP). Three hallmarks of the Macau scam are; (1) Trickster claims to be calling from a bank, the court, police or other government institution, (2) Trickster claims the victim is being investigated for alleged improprieties; and (3) To avoid victim's account being frozen, trickster persuades the victim to transfer money from their bank account and deposit it into several bank accounts.

Despite numerous warnings about the Macau scam, the public continues to fall. In 2017, the Commercial Crime Investigation Department (CCID) of Malaysian Police had reported that there were 4,500 scam cases were occurred using telephone calls and the short message service (SMS) with a total loss of RM113.11 million in 2017 ("MCPF special committee to tackle Macau Scam problem," 2019). The number of scams becomes higher each year. From January until June 2019, the CCID has received 5,069 reports on cyber-crimes involving RM250 million lost to the scammers.

From bad to worse

Aisha Riana opened her reporting file, which she will bring into the meeting room. The number of reporting incidents is much higher than a year before (Figure 1).

Aisha Riana took a deep breath and went into the meeting room halfhearted. She was afraid that what she will deliberate in the meeting will cause anger and disappointment among the board of directors, especially Datuk Syarifah Ardaniah.

Figure1: number of online fraud incidents in Mercu Suria Bank Berhad

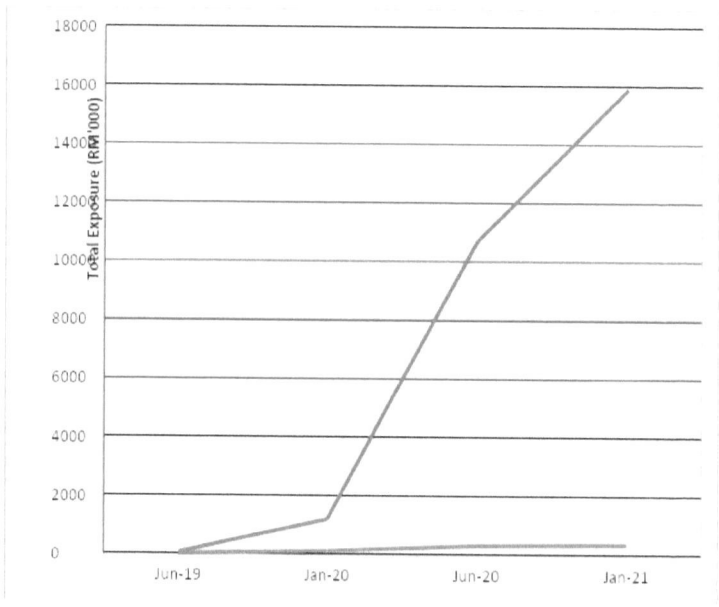

"Aisha Riana, what is your update? I hope I can see some improvements," said Datuk Syarifah Ardaniah. Aisha Riana distributed the files in her hand to all the board of directors. She explained, "In June 2019, there is ten online fraud incident's, amounting to RM4.9 thousand, reported to our department. The number of incidents is higher in the next six months after, which we received 101 incidents, which amounts to RM12 thousand". "How about this year?" Datuk Syarifah Ardaniah interrupted the conversation. "It is worst," said Aisha Riana. She can feel that Datuk Syarifah Ardaniah looks at her with her eyes wide open. "We have received a higher number of incidents, from 101 to 350 incidents", Aisha Riana continued.

"This is unacceptable!. What have you done all this while? Did you know that we just missed the opportunity to expand our client for the wealth creation business? Datuk Syarifah Ardaniah yelled at Aisha Riana. "I am sorry, Datuk. I've done my very best", Aisha Riana replied and almost cried. Datuk Syarifah Ardaniah sighed and said, "I allowed you to shine and show your potential, but you waste it. You should be aware that your failure to overcome this issue would also affect our company reputation in the eye of the public and shareholders".

Work-life does not have to be a roller coaster – what should be done?

"How was the meeting?" said Rahman to Aisha Riana. "Not going so well," replied Aisha Riana in short. "What just happened?" Rahman eagerly wants to know some feedbacks. "Datuk Syarifah Ardaniah gave me another chance. Remember Maria Arshid? The freelance risk consultant to the Malaysian government, her close friends? She wants to bring her in this company and instruct me to work with her", said Aisha Riana. "Oh, glad to hear that. I heard a lot about her and believed both of you could work well together,". Rahman replied spontaneously. "Yeah, I should be working harder from now on. Otherwise, you will never see me again in this department or this company," said Aisha Riana. She knew that she has to work harder to meet the company objective towards reducing the number of incidents. The image and reputation of MSBB could be tarnished, and her job security would be jeopardized. What should be done?

References

MCPF special committee to tackle Macau Scam problem. (2019). Bernama.

Case questions

1. What is the problem faced by Mercu Suria Bank Berhad?
2. What is the impact of online fraud in the financial sector?
3. If you were the Mercu Suria Bank Berhad director, what would your advice to Aisha Riana solve the problems?
4. If you were Aisha Riana, what are the key elements of fraud risk assessment to reduce online fraud incidents and uncertainties in the company?

CASE #3

3T's of Start-Up from Scratch: Task, Tools, and Techniques

Shathees Baskaran and David Ling Kim Hui

Introduction

"So we need to create a culture that says, start, start badly, start scrappy, make mistakes, fail and start again, but whatever you do, just start", was the voice that kept on playing in Dave's head. It was a speech from the Tedx University of Nambia by Vusi Thembekwayo, a prominent entrepreneur and venture capitalist from Africa, which he recently watched on his way to work. Looking back at his life after 15 years of working as a wage earner, it was no wonder why he felt strongly about this statement. He had been dreaming of having his own business all his life but couldn't find the time and courage for that leap of faith, as he needed the salary to pay for the bills. Only when he was handed the severance package from his company, he started to realize that his future was not as secure as he initially thought, even with a job that he perceived as stable.

On the one hand, he felt despair as the only word he could use to describe his future was bleak. On the other hand, he felt a silver lining to his situation, which made him excited. He now had more time on his hand to focus on setting up the startup company that he had been dreaming of. As the mixed thought ran through his mind, suddenly his friend Andrew, from his ex-company Quality department, called to check on him. Before they both hung up the phone, Andrew asked what plan Dave had now that he was retrenched. "I don't know", replied Dave. "I am thinking of setting up a new startup. It's a thing that I have wanted to do for a long time. There are talks about 3D printing going to be a new trend in manufacturing. I am thinking of setting a small 3D printing business, focusing on plastic components."

He knew that life as an entrepreneur could be both rewarding and risky at the same time. Few months before his retrenchment, Dave tried seeking opinions and advice from those around him on setting up a small startup, some of whom were business owners themselves. The gist of the advice that he could get was "if you believe in your gut feeling that your business idea is going to work, then find a good location and register your business with Company Commission of Malaysia" or "It's endearing that you have found the courage for the leap of faith and don't worry, if all else fail, you can always go back to the corporate world". The most encouraging advice he received was "Always remember that big companies like Apple and Dell started small. Nothing is impossible."

As much as Dave appreciated this advice, deep down, he knew that there was more to that to be an entrepreneur. He recalled the article "Five Deadly Sins of Small Business Failure" from a local online news portal at the beginning of the year. Two of the sins that he could vividly remember were lack of strategic planning and poor financial management. Dave had seen his fair share of dormant businesses or even cessation of businesses among his friends because of these 2 sins. Unfortunately, most of them jumped into the fray of entrepreneurship thinking that good business ideas and cheaper pricing were all that they needed to sustain their business, only to realize at a later stage that the quote by Benjamin Franklin "if you fail to plan, you are planning to fail" was true.

A new wind

After 15 years in the electronics device manufacturing industry, Dave had witnessed the shift of local manufacturing environment, where in the past companies were producing low technology content products, like printers and stereo systems at high lot sizes to take advantage of the economics of scale, now companies were more engaged in high technology manufacturing for industries like aerospace and semiconductor machinery, where the lot sizes were smaller but carried high value. Dave believed that his 3D printed plastic components could be an alternative to the plastic components that these companies procured, commonly produced using injection moulding and machining. However, the two commonly used production methods had a shortcoming: the former would need a bigger lot size to achieve economies of scale, and the latter would incur high wastage. Another option that Dave had was to supply to design houses and Research and Development centers. With 3D printed plastic components, Dave believed that he could offer product designers less time-consuming and cheaper alternatives as they could make do without the tool fabrication process, which would incur high cost and take weeks to complete before having a built component in their hand. This would eventually cut short the time needed to transform the conceptual design to the actual prototype. Throughout the years, Dave observed that more multinational companies had shifted their R&D centers to the Southeast Asian region, especially to Singapore. Since Dave's startup was going to be in Johor, he reckoned that he could take advantage of the proximity to Singapore to supply to these R&D centers. The third customer base that Dave could think of was those outsides of the manufacturing industry. Since 3D printing had a very wide application, he could provide 3D print souvenirs, props, models, and a host of others.

Dave was very excited about his business ideas, but the meager RM 30,000 severance package that he received from his company as a startup capital had brought him back to reality. He knew that his options for customers were very limited, and he needed to analyze his options to make the right moves thoroughly. There were two things that Dave knew for sure. The first thing was that although the main purpose of business was to make profits, the art of managing the business was cash flow management; and the second thing was that it would be naïve for Dave to expect his would-be competitors to do nothing while Dave slowly established his business and ate up their market share. Therefore, Dave needed to have a sound plan to manage his business and at the same time anticipate as well as counteract his would-be competitors' strategy. It was a sink or swim situation, and the last thing he wanted to do was fight the wrong battle and lose all of his RM 30,000 retrenchment packages if he couldn't pull this off.

The plastic machining industry

According to statistics released by Malaysia External Trade Development Association (MATRADE), 886 members or five per cent of the members were involved in the manufacturing of plastic products, with 290 members in the plastic packaging industry, 248 members in the plastic moulding industry, and 212 members in the plastic extrusion industry. There were around 40 plastic manufacturers of similar size, capabilities, and production capacity in southern Malaysia. Two of the dominant key players in the plastic injection moulding companies in Johor were Vitro & Co. and Triun & Co. Both were publicly listed companies in Bursa Malaysia.

Vitro & Co. Vitro & Co was founded in 1974 in Johor Bahru with two injection moulding machines and had grown into a company with more than 250 machines, ranging from 50 tonnes to 2,000 tonnes. For its financial year ended 31 March 2016, Vitro & Co managed to rake in more than RM 1 billion revenue. Aside from injection moulding, Vitro & Co also had its own in-house surface finishing facilities like spray painting, UV coating, silk-screen printing, and hot stamping, as well as components assembly. This made Vitro & Co be able to provide a one-stop solution for its customer. Vitro & Co was also able to capitalize on its in-depth technical expertise to provide its customer with innovative and cost-effective process design solutions, which could be translated into competitive components' prices. Vitro & Co also had in-house capabilities to design and fabricate high-precision moulds, ranging from 50 tonnes to 2,000 tonnes. All these in-house fabrication, manufacturing, surface finishing, and assembly enable Vitro

& Co not only to provide convenience to its customer but, most importantly, competitive price for its product.

Triun & Co. Triun & Co was incorporated in Malaysia in 2003 and engaged in the manufacturing and assembly of precision plastic components and fabrication of mould and died through its two wholly-owned subsidiaries. Triun & Co was owned by Seibu Corp., which was incorporated in 1978 and based in Singapore. For the financial year ended 31 December 2015, Triun & Co's revenue stood at RM 120 million. Triun & Co had various plastic injection moulding machines, which ranged from 10 tonnes to 1,300 tonnes. Aside from injection moulding and mould fabrication, Triun & Co also provided components' secondary processing services, such as spray painting, silk-screen printing, ultrasonic welding, and others, as well as an in-house component assembly to its customers.

Souvenirs given out during an event could come in many forms, from the off-the-shelf plastic trophies for the budget constraint to the hand-made silverware for those who wished to add a premium look to their souvenirs. Regardless of the type, the purpose of giving out souvenirs was as a token of appreciation to those who graced their presence in their event. Most of the souvenirs shops in southern Malaysia offered similar products, which were off-the-shelf trophies made from plastic, crystal, pewter, or aluminium.

Ferro & Co. Ferro & Co, located in Johor, Malaysia, is involved in professional corporate professional and premium gifts. It had a wide range of promotional gift items, including trophies, hanging medals, corporate gift sets, personalized stationery items, mugs, bags, and a host of others. Ferro & Co manufactured some of its products and sourced the rest from plants within the Asian region. Customers would select the type of gifts or souvenirs from this company's product list, after which the details of the events and recipients would be printed onto the souvenirs. The method that would be used to print onto the souvenirs included debossing, embossing, heat transfer printing, hot stamping, silk screen printing, laser engraving, and offset printing, all depending on the type of souvenirs chose. Ferro & Co also supply customized souvenirs but are only limited to metal or wood plaques and pendants.

Rosel & Co. Rosel & Co was founded in 1881 and had over 40 stores throughout Malaysia, with 5 stores located in southern Malaysia and exported its product worldwide through its base in Kuala Lumpur. Rosel & Co supplied over one thousand pewter-based gifts and tableware items, such as tankards, tea sets, photo frames, desk accessories, and wine accessories. Pewter was a malleable metal alloy which mainly composed of tin. It had 40 in-house designers and 250 skilled craftspeople that designed and manufactured its product line. Rosel & Co's product offerings also included glass, marble, wood, ceramic, leather, and stainless steel, which complemented its pewter product. The customer could also have their name or other particulars printed onto the pewter products that they have selected by the craftspeople, either by hand engraving or laser engraving. Aside from that, Rosel & Co also had a division where gifts and souvenirs were customized based on individual customer's preferences. Pewter products from Rosel & Co were considered a premium product with a hefty price tag compared to the average souvenirs in the market, catering to the high-end customers

The manufacturing environment

Ever since China opened up to the world at the turn of the millennia and began building its reputation as the factory of the world, many companies, including those located in the southern part of Malaysia, began to set up manufacturing plants and related supply chains in China to take advantage of its cheap labour rate. However, due to the lack of highly skilled labour in China back then, most of the products shifted to manufacturing to China were of low technology content such as entry-level printer, computer peripherals, and other consumer electronics appliances. Although the components' count in these products was low, their monthly production volume was considerably high. Factories had to run full swing, even during the weekends, to cope with the production demand. Due to the large production volume, factories were able to achieve an economy of scale. However, the gradual shift of manufacturing plants from southern Malaysia to China, especially at the beginning of the twenty-first century, caused many of the once busy roads in the industrial estate to be quiet. The production capacity for plastic injection moulding, for example, was oversupplied in the market. Although the shift in manufacturing plants didn't trigger a mass shut down of factories in southern Malaysia, it was obvious that the prospect would not be as bright as it used to be.

In response to this situation, most of the factories in southern Malaysia had no choice but to shift their focus to manufacturing high technology content products, such as lab testing equipment, medical devices, IC machines, and a host of other high component count but low volume products. Factories began to transform their conveyor assembly lines into cell production lines. They began to focus on generating savings from the economy of the scope instead of the economy of scale. It was amid this backdrop that factories began to shift from mass production to rapid prototyping. Once filled with the sound of metal stamping machines, Sheet metal fabrication factories began to invest heavily in turret punching and laser cutting machines that were more suitable for low volume production. As a result, the demand for plastic injection moulded components began to shrink and replaced by machined plastic components. The slow pick up in the economy after the 2008 financial meltdown in some way helped in the shift of the manufacturing environment to a High Mix Low Volume manufacturing environment, as companies did not only focused on the economy of scope but were also pressured to take a prudent stance in controlling its cash flow, either by renegotiating to extend the payment terms with their suppliers or to reduce the minimum order quantity of components.

The scene

The next day, Dave wasted no time planning for his new startup. After taken his breakfast, he turned on his PC and started to draft out his business plan. The first order of business for that day was to determine his startup business direction. He had in mind the main question of who would be his potential customers and what value proposition he could offer to them. Since Dave was from the manufacturing industry, he believed he could target his previous employers as his potential customer base. The shift of manufacturing environment from Low Mix High Volume to High Mix Low Volume had made it necessary for manufacturers to achieve economy of scope to sustain their business, and this was even more evident with the recent economic downturn, where customers were not only slashing down their orders due to the poor market outlook but at the same time were negotiating for a lower price for the orders that they retained. Since 3D printing was meant for low volume production, Dave reckoned that there would be demand for his service. He would have a good head start if he were to supply to this customer group since he already had on hand all the necessary business intelligence about his potential competitors, the size of their companies, their manufacturing capacity, and capability and the price that they offered.

Regardless of all the possible advantages, there was a catch to it. Dave's business would need to be minimally ISO 9001 certified for Quality Management System and other relevant certifications, depending on the application of the product that Dave was going to supply. For example, components supplied to the automobile industry would require the manufacturers to have ISO 26262 "Road Vehicle – Functional Safety" and TUV 16949 "Automobile Quality Management System" certification. Aside from that, to ensure that the components supplied met the customers' quality requirements, Dave would need to invest in special inspection equipment like Coordinate Measurement Machine (CMM), profile projectors, inspection gauges, and other tools deemed necessary by his potential customers, which would cost quite a sum of money and severely affect his business cash flow at this moment. Another consideration that Dave would need to take was the scalability of his business at this stage. Dave might not be able to promptly increase his production output to cater to the sudden increase in his customers' orders without any additional investment to increase his production capacity, which would most likely involve him purchasing additional 3D printers.

Another business segment that Dave could target was the Research and Development (R&D) centers. Previously, Dave worked with the R&D engineers during his previous employment, and he knew the challenges that these engineers faced. These R&D engineers were under pressure to validate their product design in the shortest time possible. The critical path was often the prototype components production, where these engineers had little time and margin of error. For plastic components, plastic injection moulders would take around six to eight weeks to fabricate the mould. Any design change along the way would jeopardize the R&D engineers' plan as the manufacturers would need to dismantle the tool to perform the required modifications based on the new design, which could take additional three to five working days, a time luxury that most R&D engineers didn't have. Dave believed that 3D printed components could effectively reduce the time required for R&D engineers to validate their product design by making do with the mould fabrication process and shortened the turnaround time required whenever there was any change in component design.

Since the 3D printed components would only be used to validate the R&D design and not for mass production use, Dave believed that he could do without the vigorous certification process. Aside from that, barring components that required special material to produce due to its application, most of the components in a product would be produced with the same raw material. Dave would be able to achieve economies of scope by 3D printing various components of different designs with the same raw material in one setup, an advantage that was not inherent in plastic injection moulding and plastic machining. Dave could then capitalize on these savings to offer competitive pricing to his customers. Another possibility that Dave envisioned was that few years down the road, as his business grew, he could invest in getting the necessary certifications for his business and increasing his business operation capacity and capability. Supplying prototype components to the R&D department would put his business in an advantageous position to supply components for their mass production eventually. He could capitalize on the rapport he built with the R&D and procurement team and the product knowledge he had gained along the way.

The third business segment that Dave targeted was the general public. 3D printing had a very wide application, and he could offer 3D printing services to those looking for customized souvenirs and models. Dave observed when attending any conferences or company functions that all the souvenirs given out to the guest of honor looked generic. Most of the souvenirs would look like a plaque made of plastic, wood, or tin (some with a pen holder attached) with the recipients' name engraved on it. More often than not, these souvenirs would be placed on a glass shelf in the company lobby, with other look-alike souvenirs. Dave believed that apart from being a token of appreciation, souvenirs should serve as a means to project the company image and identity, another useful tool, especially in a business-to-business marketing environment. With the appropriate finishing process, 3D printed souvenirs could look as premium as the common souvenirs available in the market.

Dave also could offer a 3D printing service to hobbyists or students who required custom-made components for their project. With the introduction of a programmable microcontroller board like

Arduino, or the low-cost multi-purpose mini-computer like the Raspberry Pi, Dave foresees that there would be demand for customized components like casing and structures from these hobbyists and students. Another possibility that 3D printing could open up was the fabrication of obsolete machine spare parts, which maintenance technicians would find very difficult to source when needed or too expensive to purchase.

The next item on his checklist was to scout for a 3D printer, the essential item for his startup operation. When it came to 3D printing plastic-based articles, there were 3 types of 3D printing technologies, namely Fused Deposition Modelling (FDM), where the workpiece was produced by heating and extruding plastic filament, stacked layer upon layer to give the 3D effect; liquid-based 3D printing, where the workpiece was produced from photosensitive liquid, hardened by a light source, with the commonly used technologies are Stereolithography (SLA), Digital Light Processing (DLP), Continuous Liquid Interface Production (CLIP), Polyjet and Multijet Printing. Finally, powder-based 3D printing, where the workpiece was produced by curing the powdered material with laser pulses, with the common technologies used, selective laser spraying (SLS) and Binder Jetting. In addition, some 3D printer technologies like Binder Jetting and Polyjet offered multi-coloured printing.

FDM was the most commonly used method for 3D modeling as it was the most affordable. The price tag for a standard FDM 3D printed ranged from less than to thousand Ringgit to tens of thousands Ringgit, depending on the speed, resolution, precision, and printable size of the printer as well as the application of the printed articles, while a standard liquid-based and powder-based 3D printer could cost upwards of ten thousand Ringgit, with liquid-based 3D printers being the most expensive among the three types. Aside from the price tag, Dave also needed to consider the operating environment and auxiliary equipment required by the 3D printers. FDM printers could be operated in an office environment, and it required filament spools to feed the filament material into the 3D printers. Both powder and liquid-based 3D printers required a special environment due to the curing method being used. On top of that, liquid-based 3D printing required a post-curing operation to strengthen the workpiece. Another consideration point that Dave needed to have was the material cost for the respective 3D printing technologies. By comparison, FDM 3D printing offered the cheapest printers and material; powder-based 3D printing had the most expensive printers and moderate material cost, while liquid-based 3D printing offered a moderate printer price but generally expensive material.

Having worked for 15 years in the procurement field, Dave instinctively knew that there would be a trade-off that he needed to seriously weigh if he chose to go with the cheaper option. Although FDM 3D printers were cheaper by comparison and more economical to operate, the quality of the workpiece produced by the FDM printers was not as detailed and as crisp as the ones produced by the powder or liquid-based 3D printing. Aesthetic-wise, liquid-based 3D printing could print workpieces with smooth finishing, while workpieces from FDM and powder-based 3D printing required additional polishing. This was an important point to take note of as secondary processes like finishing were tedious and time-consuming and would increase the production cost of the workpiece. Other considerations that Dave needed to have before purchasing the 3D printers were the printer power consumption, maintenance cost, technical support, spare parts availability, and storage condition of the raw material (be it filament, photosensitive liquid, or powdered resin). Dave would need to think these through to prevent any disruption in running his new business.

After spending the entire morning looking for appropriate 3D printers for his new startup, Dave switched his focus to finding the best location to run his daily operation. Dave initially wanted to adopt the small home office concept for his business and applied to convert his house from residential property status to business premise to save on rental but had a second thought of converting his house to a business premise would mean that he would need to fork out more for his electricity bill as the electricity tariff for commercial property was higher than those for residential property. In addition, Dave would also need to spare out a room to store all the necessary items like raw materials, which were flammable, packaging boxes, printer spare parts, and the 3D printer itself.

The economic downturn was a mixed blessing for Dave. Although he had lost his job because of it, on the flip side, it made his cost of setting up businesses relatively lower with the drop in raw material price and commercial building rental rates. Dave decided that he would rent a small shop lot for his business. He found out that the rent ranged from a few hundred Ringgit to thousands of Ringgit a month, depending on the floor space and location. He needed to find the sweet spot for his business location. The crowded area would give him good exposure to his potential client but at the same time would increase his fixed cost as the rental in these areas was expensive due to the high demand for such a space. If he decides to locate his business in the secluded area where the rental is cheap, his exposure to his potential clients would be very low, minimizing the chances of securing any business. Nonetheless, there was a silver lining to this situation. He could make up for the lack of exposure to potential clients by advertising to them directly online.

The funding

Dave already had a rough estimation of the amount of investment he would require for his startup and believed that the RM 30,000 that he had was merely enough to set up his business. After deducting all the necessary expenditures like the purchase of a unit of 3D printer, raw material, packaging boxes, as well as the two-month rental deposit for his business premise, he would be left with around RM 3,000, which was hardly enough for his business to last for 2 months. The cash flow of whatever is left after setting up his business would also need to cover his traveling expenses to the potential client site and pay the freelance 3D model technicians. Dave intuitively knew that to bid for any project successfully, and he would need to offer his potential clients attractive credit terms. To make matters worse, since he didn't have any business relationship with his material suppliers and that his business was only at its initial stage, he would need to pay them in cash whenever he got his supplies from them.

Dave had a few options to fund his new startup. First, he could open up his business to another business partner and register the business under both of their names. This would increase their initial business setup capital, which indirectly increased the business cash flow and eased the burden as running the business alone would be straining even for Dave himself. However, Dave would need to be selective in choosing his business partners. Aside from having the required business capital, the business partners would also need to be trustworthy, reliable, and have the same passion for the new business as he was. Dave was prepared not to take any salary for the first 6 months after the business inception, channelling back the supposed salary into the new business as much needed operating cash flow. He would expect his potential business partners to have the same mindset as his.

Another option for Dave was to get a bank loan to finance his business. Dave could apply to refinance his car or home mortgage. Still, the fact that he was self-employed and his business were at its startup stage would reduce his chances to get such a refinancing term and even if he could secure such a loan from the bank, the interest that he would be imposed on would not be favourable to him. Getting a personal loan would be difficult as he didn't have any collateral in the form of a tangible asset to secure the loan. Financing his business with his credit cards would also be off-limit as interest from credit card loans would be very high. Finally, Dave could try to get a Small and Medium Enterprise Micro Financing from the banks. Still, the pre-requisite for these types of financing facilities would require Dave's to submit the business track record for a minimum period of 3 years, which Dave didn't have at this moment.

Luckily for Dave, various government agencies offered credit lines to support small startup owners like him. One such credit line was the Graduate Entrepreneur Fund, a special fund to support entrepreneurship among graduates below 40 years of age. The Small and Medium Enterprise Bank (SME Bank) offered it under the Ministry of International Trade and Industry. The fund would offer financing from RM 20,000 to RM 500,000 with tenure up to 10 years and was to be used as working capital in a business incorporated in Malaysia. Another requirement for this credit line was that the applicant must attend a course conducted by the SME Bank. He had less than 2 years of business experience, a course that Dave would be more than happy to attend considering the much-needed fund injection. Aside from the Graduate Entrepreneur Fund, the alternative funding schemes were Youth Business Schemes, offered by the Ministry of Domestic Trade, Cooperative and Consumerism through Bank Kerjasama Rakyat Malaysia Berhad (BKRMB), Business Start-up Fund offered by the Ministry of Finance through Malaysia Technology Development Corporation and a host of others. The credit line offered by these government agencies came at a lower interest rate with more relaxed application criteria compared to those from the commercial banks.

The first plan

Three days went by, and Dave had gathered all the information he needed for the first part of his business plan. He had come out with a long list of possible customers and would-be competitors. Whenever he felt like getting fresh air, he would drive to the surrounding industrial area to be on the lookout for companies whose name he could populate into his list of customers. Once his business was fully set up, the first thing that Dave would do was to call up all the numbers on his potential customer list. Dave also spent hours surfing the internet, trying to absorb as much information as possible on plastic 3D printing. Other than the 3D printer's price and specification, he would also need to consider the availability of technical support for the printer.

It would be meaningless if there weren't anyone to repair the printer when it broke down.

Now Dave needed to continue with the second part of his business plan, which was the daily running of his business. "My business is new, and nobody knows who I am nor what I do. How am I going to reach out to my customers other than the ones already on my customer list?" was the first thing that popped up in his mind. Just like any new small startup, Dave didn't have the luxury of setting up a business development or marketing division in his business, nor could he afford any expensive marketing campaign. So, other than depending on his ex-colleague and friends for word-of-mouth marketing, he decided to create his business website by himself to promote his business. "I knew my programming skill would sure come in handy at moments like these", Dave thought to himself, "I think I better post my business information on all my social media account and online marketplace as well. This should increase the chances of getting customers". Dave's decision to use online channels for marketing his business was not purely due to budget constraints. Most importantly, online marketing had become a trend of late. More often than not, anyone who wished to purchase a product or service would turn to the internet, either by directly searching them through the search engine or by browsing the online marketplace like Alibaba. com or Muday.my. Dave also decided that as his business grew, he would engage a Search Engine Optimization consultant to ensure that his company's name appeared high on the list of results in the search engine whenever people were searching for a 3D printing service in Johor. This would greatly increase his business exposure to the public, thus helped in bringing new clients to him.

Reaching out to potential customers alone wouldn't bring in business for Dave. The most important thing for him was to receive an official purchase order from his customers. Dave reckoned that once his business had gained traction, he would need to spend most of his time operating the 3D printer or traveling outside to meet his customers. To not miss out on any business opportunities, especially when he was on the road, he needed to ensure that all his customers' inquiries were attended to. Hiring dedicated customer service personnel or a receptionist would be too costly for him at this stage. Upon surfing the internet, Dave came across the virtual office concept. Several small businesses operated in a shared office setup that was fully furnished, equipped with IT facilities and security. Entrepreneurs who had no access to the business premise or found it too costly to rent could register their business using the virtual office address. Aside from shared office space, the virtual office service providers also offered other value-added services such as accounting, reception services as well as goods arrangement and the amount charged by these providers could go as low as less than a hundred Ringgit per month, which was very cost-effective if compared to renting the whole business premise by himself and hiring dedicated personnel to perform these tasks. Since Dave was running a manufacturing operation, he could only use the reception and goods arrangement services. Dave would engage a delivery service provider like GDex, Poslaju, or Nationwide Express to collect the goods from the virtual office and deliver them to the intended customers.

One of the important aspects of managing an operation was tight control over the inventory, both raw material and finished goods. He needed to buy and store the right material at the right time as tied down with too much inventory would severely affect his business' cash flow and net working capital. Although he adopted the Build to Order approach, which reduced the likelihood of overstocking on finished goods, he still needed to find a robust method to control his raw material stock. Dave's 15-year experience in the procurement field had given him the necessary know-how and skill in managing the purchasing of materials. However, unlike the companies that Dave used to work for, his new startup won't be having any Material Requirement Planning suite like SAP or Oracle to help him manage his operation. Although there were cheaper alternatives developed by local IT companies, like Asoft MRP, he would need to wait for his business to grow to a certain size before investing in such a software suite. One workaround solution that he could think of was controlling his inventory by deploying the cheapest yet efficient method that he could think of and was good at, which was to use excel spreadsheets with some macro programming. Aside from controlling his material inventory, the excel spreadsheets would also be a feasible option for Dave to track his quotations to his customers, his customers' purchase order, and its fulfilment, considering the tight budget. Since Dave's business was only at its initial stage, he reckoned that the excel spreadsheet would be sufficient for him to store his sales and purchase data and perform some analysis and simple financial projections. To ensure the profitability of his business, he needed sound operation management and good cost management. One of the areas that he needed to look into was supply management. He was aware of the possible opportunity loss due to a shortage of raw material or capacity constraints of his subcontractors. Any failed delivery to his customer would be one failure too many as he would lose his customers' confidence and possible subsequent purchase orders. To ensure that he would fulfil all of his customers' orders, he needed to stock up on commonly used materials and maintain multiple supply sources for both raw material and secondary process subcontractors to mitigate the risk of raw material supply shortages or subcontractors unable to support his orders. Aside from that, having multiple supply sources would also cushion any impact of any increase in raw material or subcontractor service price as he could switch to another alternative source as he saw fit.

Dave had seen many companies go belly up throughout the years because of their inability to finance their businesses due to insufficient cash flow. Cash flow could be considered the blood in a body, without which oxygen could not be transported throughout the system. To maintain a healthy cash flow, Dave needed to be discriminative when offering payment terms and ensured that his payments were received on time. Although the notion of "the customer is always right" was held in any business, he also knew that not all customers should be treated the same way, especially when it came to payment. Therefore, he needed to clearly distinguish payment terms for the customer who placed repetitive orders and those who placed ad-hoc orders. Aside from that, Dave would also need to impose a down payment if an order reached a certain threshold to mitigate the risk and minimize loss due to customers' last-minute order cancellations or not honouring his purchase orders.

The dilemma

Two weeks later, Dave was on his way to meet his cousin, Steve, for a cup of tea. For the past few days, Dave had been busying with his new company's setup. These days went by with Dave making numerous calls to a 3D printer and material suppliers, meeting real estate agents to find the perfect location for his business, and traveling to the nearest Companies Commission of Malaysia branch to register his business. After getting the Business Registration Certificate, the next thing that Dave needed to do was to register for a current business account with a local bank. Although Dave could run his business with his account since he was running a sole propriety business, he needed to separate from his business transaction. This was particularly important as mixing the two bank transactions would make it complicated for Dave to track his business expenses and financial standings. Aside from that, by separating the two bank transactions, he could minimize the risk of missing out on any tax deduction that he was entitled to and made his business tax filing with the Inland Revenue Board of Malaysia easier.

One of the requirements to open up a current business account was for Dave to get an introducer to endorse his application. Since Steve, a businessman himself, was an account holder with this bank, Dave decided to ask for his cousin's help to be his introducer. Luckily for him, Steve was more than willing to help him out with this. As Dave was driving to Steve's office, he kept on thinking of the best way forward for his business, ways he could penetrate the market, and the possible mishaps that he might face along the way. He needed to size up the plastic manufacturing market and his would-be competitors to minimize the risk of getting into the wrong business and, at the same time, plan for future competencies that he would need to build for his business to survive in the long run. Suddenly, Dave had a flashback of the speech that he heard in a Tedx talk. There were four levels of entrepreneurs; startup, survivalist, success, and growth. "What are survivalists? I need money at month end to pay my bills. How do you know you are one? It is usually one person with three, maybe four people in his team. He is operating in a small office and is just barely making it. Every month you must make money to pay for the month's bill." Many businesses died at the instance in which they became survivalists.

Dave's main priority now was to focus his energy to move his business from survivalist to success and eventually growth level, as quick as he could. He knew that it was easier said than done. That was why he could not afford to make any mistake now that he had his business setup. Dave had yet to place an order for the 3D printers and needed to decide soon as it would determine the type of 3D printers he would need to purchase, the first big-ticket item for his business.

Case questions

1. Weigh internal and external factors and defend Dave's intention to set up a new startup business.
2. Suggest potential business options for Dave.
3. Recommend an appropriate business direction to Dave. Assess associated business risks and conceive a risk management plan.

CASE #4

Don't Be A Copycat, Designers!

Ebtihal Ebrahim and Haliyana Khalid

Prologue

After a long week of doing a lot of projects, Toola decided to take a short break. She likes achievements feelings; therefore, whenever she accomplished any of her targets, she rewards herself. This time, a few days ago, she designed a project that will be distributed to a national level, and she was so proud of that. She was reading one of her favourite books with a warm cup of coffee when she suddenly received an unexpected phone call. It was the client of that project, but she was not happy, which was clear from her voice tone. *'Is the design you did for me yours?'* she asked in a loud voice.

Toola did not understand at the beginning what was going on. She was confused, and she thought that maybe she did send the wrong email. So, she replied, *'Yes, it is mine, what is wrong?'*

The client explained to her that someone else just published the same design after a few days of the original submission day of

Toola's, but with a different signature and designer name on it. And she wanted an explanation from Toola.

The history of graphic design

Since the early nations, people were looking and appreciating visual beauty, whether it is natural such as the color of the sky, the clouds, the trees, and the sea, or it is some of the artwork that was done by human beings such as the artwork that done by the ancient Egyptians thousands of years ago.

From that time till today, people still have the same principles of art. Any type of art has some elements, such as lines, dots, and shapes -like circles and rectangles-. Also, all arts share the same principles about coloring and matching. From that, it is understood that all types of art share the same idea of collecting the information, organizing the data, and explaining the ideas in pretty and attractive ways. One of the most popular arts right now is "Graphic Design". Some history books have used illustrations such as drawing life examples of natural elements like flowers, tree leaves, and so on; just a few copies of those books have survived so far. But it shows evidence of the illustrations that have been used in the old books. Most of that books were in Britain and Europe. In Islamic countries, during history, they used graphic design, especially in writing the Arabic letters in the Holy Qur'an. The Muslim scientists used black ink on golden paper; some of that golden paper is from real gold, and others just the color is gold. They used to write in an angled alphabet called "Alkufi", one of the famous fonts in writing Arabic letters. Most of this writing started in the eighth century and reached its peak in the 10th century. After done with writing the Holy Qur'an, Muslims began to add some unique decorations around the text; on the margins of each page, this graphic technique was added to make the appearance of the book prettier and more attractive. Later in the 12th century, the next alphabet invented was the "Naqsh" alphabet, which is different a little bit from "Alkufi", but both are from the basic Arabic fonts today. (Drogin 1980)

Copyrights

Copyright Ó is world widely known as the legal right of the original creator of a certain work. It gave the creator the right to establish their roles on using the work, such as; copy, publish, edit, and use. It is mainly for the creative kind of work, such as the idea of a design or a story of a novel. For example, if anyone wanted to create a movie based on a novel, it is necessary to take the author's permission and follow the copyrights regulations. Otherwise, it will be a crime to carry on without permission from the original author.

In the graphic design aspect, it means to allow others to use any content of a design and under which circumstances. For example, a flyer design which is available online for anyone to download and use for free, but the designer commented that it allows for personal use only, this means if someone used it for commercial use, they are committing a legal offence and the original creator of the design can sue them by the use of the copyrights law.

The culture of the copyrights is not well established and known in some regions, such as the developing countries. Therefore, it is very important for the individuals who seek to protect their work and ideas to be aware of it and the users who should not violate other's rights just because they know how to do that.

Copyrights are not only for the individuals, but it is also applicable in organization's level. Software companies such as Microsoft and Adobe are also concerned about copyrights issues. With internet sources nowadays, it is easy to install any of their software without paying or having a legal license. Each software or product can be used for a few days as a trial period then the user is required to pay a certain price to use it legally for a lifetime or a certain period. This depends on the company's policy. For example, for the individual's package in Adobe, having a one-year subscription for 3 apps (Lightroom CC, Lightroom Classic CC, Photoshop CC) with a 1TB of cloud storage cost $239,88. While for a single app such as (illustrator), it cost the same amount as the 3 apps. This deference is because of the unique features of each app (See Figure 1).

Figure 1
Adobe Software Prices (Example)

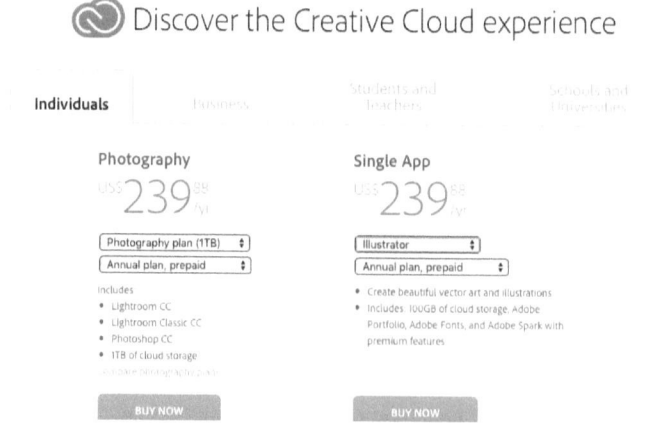

On the other hand, some people have those applications for free. Just because they know how to hack. There are many reasons for the need of having strong copyright laws, as well as distributing the culture among the community, such as:

1. Weak laws in the past, when the beginning of the spread of technology in the world.
2. The low sales rate of technical products from owners.
3. Ensure copyright of tampering users of modern technologies.

Hacking and software cracking

Hacking, in general, means having an unauthorized intrusion into an electronic device such as computers, mobile phones, or networks. The person responsible for doing any of these activities is known as a hacker. The hacker can change any feature inside the hacked system such as; passwords and security to change the behavior or the target of that system and make it respond to the hacker commands.

Hacking sometimes can be used for good purposes, but it all depends on the hacker's intention and the circumstances. Software cracking means making software changes to remove or disable some of its features, essential to protect the content. For example, cracking removes the passwords, serial numbers, or sometimes the disabled copy feature. In other words, cracking helps the user use the software without having a permeation or a license from the developer, which means basically "Stealing".

The first software copy protection was the one Apple company developed for Apple II, released in 1977. The main objective of this software was to stop unauthorized copying of software. Then, continuous development efforts were conducted by all IT companies, which resulted in the high and secure protection that we have today.

Freelancer's life

Since Toola started her working career, she had different experiences. From that, she came up with so many different backgrounds. For her first job, she began to be a trainee in an administration office. That office did not pay for her; she decided to be trained voluntarily to get to know people better and have working experience. At that time, she was just 15 years old, she used to go to school in the morning, and in the afternoon, she goes to her job to work, and at night she had some time to do her homework for school. Many years after that, she developed so many skills such as; she has memorized the Holy Qur'an, having most of the secretarial skills and having basic ideas about designing software and applications, and much more.

After a little bit of time, she started to have her designs. The first design she made was a project for her morning school. She still remembers that project clearly. All her teachers appreciated it, and she even gets rewarded for it. Since then, she was so excited to learn more about graphics, only by herself. Whenever she had free time, she opens the designing programs and then uses any tools to learn more. Her approach to learning was by practising and making mistakes. Meanwhile, she was also still having her administrative work besides the morning school, and she added the graphic designing talent; yes, she began to realize that it is her talent, and she has a huge passion for it. Whenever she sees a good design anywhere, for example: in the streets, a magazine, or even online, she wondered how she could do such a good design like professional designers do.

Graphic designing as a profession

From the zero points that she had no idea about graphic designing, she started to feel that she has a talent for drawing on the computer, even though her drawing on paper is not that good. However, still, she can do some sketches for her to draw after that on the computer. She can do digital drawing and artwork, but not by using paper and pen in traditional ways. She started to learn the professional designing programs, especially the Adobe Photoshop program, on her own; then, she got help from her siblings (Abdulrahman, Iman). Just to have some simple designing technics such as: merging photos with some texts. After a while, she understood some principles about the coloring, the basic shapes, the things that can be merged, how to use the brush inside the designing software, etc. Later, some people saw her work, and they were amazed by it. They like each piece of her work. One of them asked her to do a special logo design for a certain project, and that was her first client. From that, she started a new search for a new field which is logo designing. She had done her first logo for that friend for free, but she learned something special and new.

A few months later, she started to sell her designs after she gains some confidence; which means she started her career as a graphic designer without knowing what was the meaning of being a freelancer -yet-. She started to sell her designs one by one. After that, customers came to her to ask for a specific customized design; then, when she finishes the design, she submits it to the customer, but she did not give prices for anything. She just let the customers price the designs of what they think is suitable for her work.

After a while, when she became a professional in doing her work and having more business knowledge, she started her freelancing career. So, it was very clear with special agreements with each client. Right now, she is a professional graphic designer. She also travelled to Egypt to study graphic designing diploma in all graphics programs such as Adobe Photoshop, Adobe Illustrator, Adobe In design, etc. Also, she had a motion graphics diploma for all videos and montage programs such as Adobe after Effects, Adobe Premiere, Cinema 4D, and 3-D studio max… etc.

Right now, she is working as a freelance graphic designer and motion graphic designer as well. She has a special team that she is working within the projects that need a team, but most of her work are individual designs that she designs herself, and 100% of her work is original work which means it is all hers from the zero points till the end of the project.

Stealing issue

In 2015, Toola was required to do a flyer design for a client from the ministry of education in Saudi Arabia. This design was for an educational prize for many educational levels, in particular, three different levels: first, administration's level, second, supervisor's level, third, teacher's level.

Normally, when she started any design, she starts by drawing sketches using a pencil and white blank paper. Still, sometimes, she does start by drawing the design on the computer using any designing app like Photoshop. In this case, she started by imagining the design then, doing some sketches by drawing with hand. When she has done all drawing stagers on drafts, she implemented the design using Adobe illustrator designer. In this particular app, the best thing to do is to start by drawing the basic shapes altogether, not to use the built-in shapes, and this was the technique that she used in this particular design. Because she likes to have always unique designs that even the used shapes on them are completely new based on her ideas and art. And this is what makes her designs famous, and many clients want to work with her because of that and the trust feeling they get working with her.

After creating the design, she contacted the client to submit the design for her in both: printed and soft copy, as they had agreed when they signed the job in the first place. What happened at that time is, after she did with the flyer and submitted it to the client, suddenly, after a few days they called her back -the client particularly- she was angry, and she started to ask about the design she asked *'are you the one who designed this flyer?'*. At the very beginning, Toola didn't understand what she means so, and she asked her, 'What's *going on?'*. Then, she said that someone else today published the same design but with different colors and the same content! And she thought that Toola might give the same design to 2 different clients!

In the designing's world, we cannot say if this design is original unless we are experts or working with the legal designing fields. Therefore, the only proof that Toola can show to the client was that she was the one who submitted this design first on the date of her submission. After that, the other designer from another state just took her design, changed the colors, removed her signature, put their signature, submitted the design, and finally published it.

Another unique service that Toola provided for her customers upon request is content writing. And luckily for this flyer, she was the one who wrote the content too, and the other designer -who steal her work- also had taken the same content.

Only from this experience, since it was her first time facing a situation like that, she understood how important it is to know how to protect her designs and idea, and she also knew what it means to steal other's works in graphic design fields.

There are millions of free designs on the internet, and some of these designs are stolen from the original designer who creates them. But it is published without the copyrights from the designer themselves. Unfortunately, in so many countries so far, they don't consider this stealing as a crime so, in 2015, when someone stole Toola's original work and put their signature on it, she couldn't do anything. she couldn't sue this person to get her rights back because no one considered this as a crime -as far as she knew-. Nowadays, the government, too, is paying attention to this kind of crime, and they consider it real stealing, and people can go to the judge if they have any problems with electronic crimes.

Another hard experience which has been heard from one of the famous designers -whom Toola learned a lot from-she said:

> "last few months, I was robbed from the "Behance. net" site by an advertising company, which was very bad. I learned about it through a follower who sent me the link to the company that displayed

my works on its homepage from within its business. This made me embarrassed even in front of customers. I sent an email to that company asking them to delete my designs from their page. I waited for two days and did not get a response. On the third day, the designs were deleted from the page, but I did not get an apology, and I they did not explain why!"

(Khansaa Abo-Naji 2017)

A famous quotation that Pablo Picasso said: "***Good designers copy***", which some misunderstood and take as literally as it is without understanding the actual meaning. Good designers copy means seeing others' work as inspiration and learning from them. The quote was never meant for designers to steal or to copy the ideas 100%. But it is so much helpful to see and explore the details behind the great designs and art. By this, a greater idea can be generated. Therefore, great designs are considered an important part of the inspiration.

Furthermore, she came out with some more lessons. A knowledge that she just realized after this experience, she did understand what it means to steal someone's work. So, she started to be more careful when using any open source from any online source or website. So, she pays so much attention to the copyrights. If it is not a free source, she has to pay for it even if she can hack to have it. She understands the principles of purchasing or just cracking the design programs; before that experience, she didn't realize that working on cracked programs is forbidden (haram) in Islam so, from that day till today, she never use cracks with any programs, she only use the original license which positively affects her job, and she could feel the blessing since.

Another thing that she had to change after that experience was her pricing strategy. She understands how she can price her original work, so she begins to price her work professionally. It appears that so many designers out there just take other people's designs and change them a little bit. Then, they sell these designs to the clients. By this, they are cheating, and they don't make a real effort to do the designs. So, their designs are so much cheaper than hers her designs are all original, and it is all her work and ideas, so she knows the price of her designs must be high. She must say this to the clients, so they understand that all of her work is original and it is just for this client she never does the same design to 2 clients.

Another challenge she faced after that was accepting her prices since there are many designers in the market, and their pricing is cheaper than hers. Some of her regular clients dropped the work with her because of that, but they all respected her point of view. She struggled to get it all her way, but she had a strong motive and a strong determination to do only what she believes in, no matter if all the people around are doing it differently. The signature also is very important. In the past, she didn't pay much attention to putting her name or her signature on her designs, but she never published any of her designs without her signature on them after a while. Also, she and the client both have to agree on this while signing the working contract and agreements. Writing a contract before starting the design is also another technic that she implemented after several years of working experience. She must have a contract that proves that she had submitted the work to the client and they agree on all the work that she does and the guarantee that all the work is her work and it is all original. By this, she does explain herself clearly, and the clients gain more trust feeling and professionalism. Trying to be ethical nowadays actually is difficult, and not so many people understand or appreciate that. There are so many freelancers worldwide, which makes a huge competition, especially in terms of pricing. Most of those freelancers are using non-licensed programs so, and they are using the programs for Free, which means they don't pay anything to the designing programs and websites which Toola does pay for. So, their designs are much cheaper than her designs. Because of that, when she agreed with a new client, she clarifies that her work is legal and all of her programs are original and legally licensed, and all the designs she creates are 100% her work.

This is not the only issue that people face in this industry. Much more challenges and difficulties are facing Toola as a freelance graphic designer. So, should she continue the same pricing and approaches? Or should she follow what others are doing in the same industry?

Case questions

1. Draw a business model for the freelance graphic designer.
2. To understand the journey of a freelance designer, draw a road map of the designing projects.
3. What are the advantages and disadvantages of the approach that Toola has taken? What are your recommendations to her?
4. What are the key takeaways from the case

CASE #5

Ayub Seafood Bangi: Which Way To Go?

Adriana Mohd. Rizal, Nomahaza Mahadi, Ong Choon Hee and Suzilawati Kamarudin

Introduction

One evening in March 2016, En. Izam Mohamed (subsequently known as En. Izam) sat quietly in his office and was deep in thoughts, planning for his next move. He owned and ran a family restaurant, Ayub Seafood Bangi (subsequently known as AS Bangi), which he established in October 2011 with an investment of RM900,000. AS Bangi main dish was a home recipe for grilled fish with *petai*. Since its opening, AS Bangi had recorded sales growth for three consecutive years: 15 per cent in 2012, 20 per cent in 2013 and 25 per cent in 2014. En. Izam was grateful that all his hard work and sleepless nights were paid off. Nonetheless, an important event that took place almost two years ago still haunting him until the present day. He remembered vividly the moment he learnt about the news that AS Bangi's land lease might not be renewed. He panicked. Never once in his life had he felt that way if the land lease was not renewed, AS Bangi would abruptly cease operation.

It all started when he received a phone call from the landowner, CDSH Sdn. Bhd. (subsequently known as CDSH), sometimes in June 2014.

En. Izam:	Hello, this is Izam from Ayub Seafood Bangi.
Officer:	Hello En. Izam, I'm Razak from the CDSH office.
En. Izam:	Hello En. Razak. How are you?
Officer:	I am fine, thank you. I call to inform you that your renewal application is put on hold now.
En. Izam:	May I know why?
Officer:	I am sorry, En. Izam. CDSH is in the midst of discussion. We will let you know once everything is concluded.

He could not forget the conversation he had with the CDSH officer. His body trembled the minute the conversation ended. Filled with anxiety, En. Izam then called company advisor, Pn. Naura.

En. Izam:	I just received a call from the CDSH officer regarding the leasing renewal application.
Puan Naura:	Great! Are they going to renew the lease?
En. Izam:	I'm afraid not. CDSH is keeping our application on hold.
Puan Naura:	Oh no… What do you plan to do?
En. Izam:	I do not know… but I believe it is time for AS Bangi to find its own place.

After that conversation, En. Izam had a few more meetings with Pn. Naura. Since the establishment, AS Bangi was operating on a lease land owned by CDSH. En. Izam had signed four years lease agreement, and he had about a year to find a new location of AS Bangi before the lease expired in June 2015. In his thought, he believed he could find and secure a new business location by December 2014. If the lease was not renewed, he figured he had enough time to move out to a new place.

Malaysian food service industry

The Malaysian lifestyles had changed increasingly due to long working hours. Consequently, their eating pattern also changed. They favoured fast food and food delivery services as it was convenient and less time-consuming. This was the reason for the rise of a drive-through facility, home delivery, and takeaway. The changing lifestyle also created a demand for quick and convenient dining such as cafes and delis. This trend had ultimately changed the landscape of the Malaysian food service industry.

The danger of diabetes and obesity had also influenced the Malaysian dietary. Menus with balanced nutrients were sought after, which impacted the future sales of full-service restaurants and cafes. Halal food also played an important factor. As Malaysia was becoming a Halal hub in the region, food service operators and manufactures must comply with halal standards and requirements (Halal Industry Development Corporation, March 2014).

The growth of the Malaysian economy with a value of US$316.2 billion in 2013 had an impact on food service and food service establishment. The high workforce and long work hours also pressed for fast food services. This trend had supported the growth of the Malaysian food service market that was estimated at just below US$10 billion in 2012 (Table 1). In addition, densely populated areas like Klang Valley were homes for Malaysian and foreigners had created more demand for a variety of food service establishments to cater for a diverse consumer base (Euromonitor, 2014).

Even though chain operators saw increased sales and growth, independent food service operators dominated the industry. While full-service restaurants remained a key sector, café and home delivery/takeaway showed growing sales, outlets, and transactions since 2008. This trend was expected to continue to 2017 (Euromonitor, 2014).

Malaysian food service subsectors comprised full-service restaurants, fast food, cafés, street stalls, food kiosks, cafeterias, and home delivery/takeaway only. With a total sale of US$10 billion in 2012, the number was expected to reach US$13 billion in 2017 (Table 1). As a result, the compound annual growth rate (CAGR) was estimated to expand to 5.3 in 2017 from 4.6 in 2012. Full-service restaurant was the dominant Subsector in 2012, representing over one-third of the total market. Nevertheless, the fastest growing Subsector was delivery/takeaway with 19.9 CAGR between 2008 to 2012 (Euromonitor, 2014).

Table 1 Historic and Forecast Market Value and Growth of Malaysian Food Service by Subsector

Historic Market Value and Growth of Malaysian Foodservice by Subsector, US$ millions

	2008	2009	2010	2011	2012	CAGR % 2008-12
Consumer Foodservice	8,358.8	8,519.2	8,984.3	9,503.2	9,989.9	4.6
Full-Service Restaurants	3,013.5	3,016.1	3,135.1	3,297.0	3,428.3	3.3
Cafés/Bars	2,427.2	2,472.5	2,593.0	2,719.8	2,869.8	4.3
Street Stalls/Kiosks	1,724.1	1,750.8	1,837.2	1,929.4	2,015.5	4.0
Fast Food	995.7	1,063.9	1,186.5	1,309.6	1,415.4	9.2
Self-Service Cafeterias	166.5	173.1	180.3	188.8	195.3	4.1
100% Home Delivery/Takeaway	31.8	42.8	52.1	58.7	65.6	19.9
Pizza Consumer Foodservice**	174.4	190.5	207.4	220.6	230.9	7.3

Forecast Market Value and Growth of Malaysian Foodservice by Subsector, US$ millions

	2013	2014	2015	2016	2017	CAGR % 2013-17
Consumer Foodservice	10,511.2	11,064.4	11,648.7	12,275.5	12,939.1	5.3
Full-Service Restaurants	3,594.8	3,779.6	3,975.1	4,191.5	4,431.3	5.4
Cafés/Bars	3,027.4	3,186.8	3,353.4	3,527.5	3,707.1	5.2
Street Stalls/Kiosks	2,098.2	2,189.9	2,292.2	2,405.9	2,529.5	4.8
Fast Food	1,513.2	1,614.3	1,718.0	1,823.5	1,929.1	6.3
Self-Service Cafeterias	204.1	211.7	219.4	229.2	237.1	3.8
100% Home Delivery/Takeaway	73.5	82.1	90.6	97.9	105.0	9.3
Pizza**	243.8	258.1	273.3	288.0	303.9	5.7

Source for both: Euromonitor, 2014. CAGR = compound annual growth rate.
**Pizza consumer foodservice data is compiled from three different subsectors (fast food, full-service restaurants, and 100% home delivery/takeaway) for the purposes of comparison, but remains reflected within the figures for these subsectors, and thus the consumer foodservice total. As such, pizza is not counted as its own sector within the consumer foodservice total.

Full-service restaurants

Full-service restaurants serving Asian cuisine remained the main food service subsectors in Malaysia. However, a full-service restaurant serving western food was also on the rise over the 2008-2012 periods. The growing popularity of western food was stemmed from the strong branding of international brands and high consumers' interest. As a result, full-service restaurants accumulated sales of US$3.4 billion and recorded a CAGR of 3.3 per cent between 2008 and 2012. In 2012, full-service restaurants averaged US$335,089 in sales per outlet and US$12.71 per transaction. For the forecast period of 2013 and 2017, full-service restaurants are estimated to reach US$4.4 billion in sales with a CAGR of 5.4 per cent. However, heavy discounts and promotions could dampen overall growth in this Subsector.

Shah Alam market

Shah Alam was only 25 kilometres away from Kuala Lumpur, the Malaysian capital. Shah Alam city covered 290.3 square kilometres with 650,000 people in 2014 (MBSA, 2016). 77 per cent of Shah Alam population were Malays, 13 per cent were Chinese, eight per cent Indian, and two per cent were others (Department of Statistics Malaysia, 2015).

Shah Alam was an industrial city with a modern infrastructure. Generally, Shah Alam was divided into the north, central, and south parts (refer to Exhibit 10). Altogether, Shah Alam had 64 sections; North Shah Alam consisted of 18 sections; the Central Shah Alam consisted of 24 sections; the South Shah Alam consisted of 12 sections.

There were several shopping malls in Shah Alam, including AEON Shah Alam, Plaza Alam Sentral, SACC Mall, Plaza Shah Alam, Ole-Ole, Anggerik Mall and PKNS Complex. The commercial areas were located at Seksyen 14, Seksyen 13 and Seksyen 9. Universiti Teknologi MARA (UiTM) was the only public university in Shah Alam. There were also other private higher learning institutions such as Universiti Industri Selangor (UNISEL), Management and Science University (MSU), and PTPL College. There were also a few industrial-related education centres such as Shah Alam Polytechnic, CIAST, and ADTEC in Shah Alam.

There were many eatery places in Shah Alam, and they were owned mainly by Muslims. Some of the famous restaurants in Shah Alam were Pak Su Corner Restaurant (Malay food), Grease (western food), Zam Zam Arabic (Arabic food), Orkid Thai (Thailand), Pecel Lele (Indonesia), Gangnam Station Restaurant (Korean cuisine) and Adam Lai Restaurant (Chinese cuisine). In Shah Alam, there were also a few established grilled fish and seafood restaurants, such as Ikan Bakar Maju, Restoran Arang Ikan Bakar, Mee Ketam Restaurant and Jemari Restaurant.

Bangi market

Bandar Baru Bangi township was crowned as "Knowledge City" in 2008 by the Selangor Chief Minister. Bandar Baru Bangi was surrounded by several higher learning institutions, such as Universiti Kebangsaan Malaysia (UKM), Universiti Tenaga Nasional (UNITEN), Universiti Putra Malaysia (UPM), and Universiti Multimedia (MMU). Moreover, Bandar Baru Bangi was only 12 kilometres away from Kajang – a well-known city for its grilled meats - *satay*. In addition, Bandar Baru Bangi was located next to Putrajaya – the federal administrative capital - and about 25 km away from Kuala Lumpur. Bandar Baru Bangi area covered 7,228 acres and consisted of 16 sections (see Exhibit 11) with a population of more than 100,000 in the year 2014.

Section 16 in Bandar Baru Bangi was an industrial area housed many multinational manufacturing companies such as Sony, Hitachi, Upha, Sapura, Onkyo, and Denso. The commercial areas were in Section 1, Section 4, Section 7, Section 8 and Section 9.

Bandar Baru Bangi had old and new shopping malls. The old shopping complexes were PKNS complex and Warta Mall (now KiP Mall). The new ones were Bangi Gateway and Bangi Sentral. Bandar Baru Bangi was also home to famous boutiques like Butik Ariani, Butik Qalesha, Butik Siti Khadijah, Tudung Fareeda, and Al-Ikhsan.

Bandar Baru Bangi had several exotic eatery places. There was a good mix of full-service restaurants of Malay, western, Arabic, Indonesian, Korean, Japanese, Italian and Chinese. Some of the famous restaurants were Red Card Cafe (Western and Italian food), Restoran Nasi Ulam (Malay food), Restoran Wong Solo (Indonesia cuisine), D' Limau Nipis (Malay food), Al Diafah Express (Arabic cuisine), Midori Japanese Restaurant (Japanese Cuisine) and Mohd Chan Restaurant (Chinese cuisine).

Firm formation and initial business development

En. Izam was the owner and lead entrepreneur of AS Bangi, an enterprise company. He graduated in 1998 with a degree in Technology Management from Universiti Teknologi Malaysia (UTM). Upon graduation, he worked with Tamura Electronics Sdn. Bhd. as Quality Control Executive for four years before he joined T&K Autoparts Sdn. Bhd. as a Quality Assurance and Quality Control Executive in 2002. In 2005, he found new employment with Nichicon (M) Sdn. Bhd. as a Quality Assurance and Quality Control Executive. After three years, he resigned from his work and moved to the United Kingdom. His wife pursued her doctoral study at Southampton University. In Southampton, En. Izam managed to find a few part-time jobs to supplement his wife study allowances. In 2011, after his wife completed her study, En. Izam and his family returned to Malaysia. They decided to settle down in Bangi. En. Izam decided to open another branch for his family food business, Ayub Seafood, in Bangi.

In June 2011, En. Izam received an offer from CDSH to rent vacant land in Seksyen 16, Bangi. There were also police and fire stations nearby. The location was just 200 metres from the Bangi/UKM toll booth (see Exhibit 1 location search AS Bangi via Google map). Close to North-South Expressway, the location was accessible to both local and other nearby customers. With a population of about 30,000 people (Selangor Town and Country Planning Department, 2010) and surrounded by residential areas, multinational factories, government agency offices (police stations, fire stations, district office, Department of Irrigation and Drainage) and other institutions and private companies (National University of Malaysia, Universiti Putra Malaysia, Universiti Tenaga National, Malaysia France Institute and several other private colleges and universities), gave AS Bangi, a large base of potential customers.

En. Izam used his saving and borrowed money from his family members, close friends and bank when he established AS Bangi in October 2011. Initially, AS Bangi had a seating capacity of 400. A roof sheltered about 60 per cent of the seating area, and about 40 per cent was an open space (refer to Exhibit 2 to Exhibit 4). In addition, there were prayer rooms for men and women, a kid's playground (refer to Exhibit 5) and toilets. Furthermore, a ramp for the disabled was built in addition to a special parking bay. The customers' parking space in AS Bangi could accommodate 100 cars at one time (refer to Exhibit 6). AS Bangi operating hours were from 5 pm to 12 am daily.

In the beginning, AS Bangi had 32 workers, including cooks, porters and waiters. All AS Bangi workers were local citizens. 60

per cent of the workers were En. Izam's relatives. Paying higher than the market salary, AS Bangi also offered various incentives such as Employee Provident Fund (EPF), Social Security Organisation (SOCSO), bonus, and allowances. EPF provided retirement benefits for members through their savings management efficiently and reliably (EPF, 2012), while the SOCSO scheme provided two social security schemes, namely the Employment Injury Scheme and the Invalidity Scheme (SOCSO, 2015). The Employment Injury Scheme protected employees against contingencies, including occupational disease and accidents that occurred while travelling during employment. On the other hand, the Invalidity Scheme provided 24 hours' coverage against invalidity or death due to any cause (SOCSO, 2015).

The first two years were the most challenging time for En. Izam. He spent most of his time at the restaurant to oversee the business operation. For example, at one time, AS Bangi could not get enough sugar and cooking oil supply because they were limited in the market. At that time, AS Bangi did not have reliable suppliers. Managing the staff was another challenge. En. Izam had to ensure that the workers were motivated and always at their best to serve the customers. To motivate them, En. Izam rewarded the staff financially with monthly performance bonuses, annual bonuses, holidays, schooling aids, non-interest personal loans, and other perks. By the end of 2012, AS Bangi had an additional area for private functions with a capacity of 100 seatings. In December 2013, AS Bangi had grown rapidly and managed to attract customers from other areas like Gombak, Shah Alam, Klang and Seremban. Some of the customers were even from Melaka and Johor. As a result, AS Bangi annual sales grew by 15 per cent in 2012 and 20 per cent in 2013.

AS Bangi unique business philosophy

Amongst AS Bangi unique philosophies was its Syariah-compliant business practices. Following Syariah Law, En. Izam avoided offering any products or services that were prohibited by Islamic principles. As such, female staff were required to cover their hair, perform prayers, and prevent corruption. Another AS Bangi's business philosophy was to offer fresh and quality fish at affordable prices.

Ayub Seafood - The parent company

The idea to grill fish with *petai* was originated from Mak Ana crave for *petai*. Mak Ana is En. Izam's eldest sister. She mixed *petai* in her recipes, and it became a favourite among their customers. *Petai, scientifically* known as Parkia Speciosa, has long, flat edible beans with bright green seeds the size and shape of plump almonds, which have a rather peculiar smell. Parkia Speciosa is well-known in Southeast Asian countries like Indonesia, Malaysia, Singapore, Thailand, and Laos (HealthBenefitTimes.com, 2016). *Petai* is rich in carbohydrates and dietary fibre, where the seeds contained high amounts of complex carbohydrates. Petai also enhanced the heart and digestive system (Health Remedy, 2016).

The establishment of Ayub Seafood restaurant was dated back to 1997. The completion of Abu Bakar bridge construction in 1997 that linked Tanjung Lumpur and Kuantan had opened a new chapter to the community socio-economic development. Since the opening of the new bridge, Tanjung Lumpur became a popular destination for fresh seafood from the surrounding communities and outside Kuantan. Seeing the opportunity, Mak Ana rushed to open a family restaurant.

On April 14, 2003, Mak Ana registered her restaurant as *Ayub Ikan Bakar dan Tomyam* and adopted the brand name Ayub Seafood (AS). She later registered the brand name as a company trademark in 2015. AS Bangi's main business was to offer fresh seafood cuisine. It also offered a variety of dishes and hot soups. The most popular dish was grilled fish with *petai*. The fish was grilled with a spicy sauce and sliced *petai*. AS Bangi used a traditional technique to grill. The fish was wrapped with banana leaf and grilled using charcoal. Due to requests, AS Bangi also provided catering services to private individuals, government departments, the private sector, charities, *surau* and mosques.

Besides grilled fish and seafood, AS Bangi also made the local delicacy such as *satar, otak-otak, keropok lekor* (refer to Figure 1), and dried and salted fish. *Satar* is a mixture of blended fish meat, black pepper, grated coconut, chillies, shallots, and ginger. The mixture is then wrapped in a coned shaped banana leaf. Several *satar* are pierced together with a bamboo stick and grilled above charcoal fire (Terengganu Tourism, 2016). *Satar* is a famous appetiser at AS Bangi Tanjung Lumpur, and on average, 600 pieces of *satar* were sold every day. *Otak-otak* is another traditional appetiser from Terengganu. It is a snack made from processed fish meat. Otak-otak is marinated fish slices soaked in a thick spice coating made from minced shallots, onions, ginger, and chillies. They are then wrapped with coconut leaves and cooked over a slow charcoal fire (Tourism Terengganu, 2011). *Keropok Lekor* is also another popular snack, and it is fish meat sausage. *Keropok lekor* is made of de-boned fish, such as sardine, *ikan tamban (sardine-like fish)*, herring or *ikan kerisi*.

Ikan selayang is the popular choice as it has a sweet taste. Mixed with sago flour, it is then kneaded into a long dough and boiled for several hours. The long doughy rolls are then sliced into bite-sized chunks and deep-fried until golden brown. Eating it hot with a special dipping chilli sauce has undoubtedly made it a popular snack time choice (Tourism Malaysia, 2016).

Satar *Otak-otak* *Keropok Lekor*

Figure 1   Local Snacks (*Satar*, *Otak-otak* and *Keropok Lekor*)

In July 2010, AS Bangi opened its second branch on the side of the main road, which connected Tanjung Lumpur and Pekan town. Subsequently, in October 2011, AS Bangi opened its third branch in Bangi. The fourth branch was opened in July 2014 and is located just next to the AS Bangi main branch in Tanjung Lumpur. The fourth branch was the biggest among AS Bangi branches and could accommodate up to 700 people at one time. Another RM 0.9 million was invested in pushing AS Bangi as a premier home recipe restaurant for grilled fish. At the fourth branch, a kiosk measured 20 feet by 10 feet was built to sell local products, such as fish crackers, salted fish (refer to Exhibit 7), and other marine products. A total of 60 local workers were recruited and trained in cooking, management, and finance. The premise was already being featured in a number of TV shows, magazines and selected as a host location for TV9's Best in Town show (refer to Exhibit 8 and Exhibit 9).

Business growth

In early 2014, the number of AS Bangi customers had grown, and it had 52 full-time workers to serve 700 customers at any one time. In addition, during the weekends or public holidays, AS Bangi would hire another 6 to 10 part-time workers. With the expanding workforce, AS Bangi paid around RM80,000 a month on salary for its full-time workers. AS Bangi also invested RM120,000 to upgrade its facilities, such as a covered dining area, expanded praying area, extra toilets and improved landscape.

AS Bangi supplies were directly sourced from Pasar Borong Selayang. En. Izam would fetch the fish and seafood supplies after midnight to ensure their freshness and quality. In addition, for weekends or festive times, En. Izam would buy 30 per cent more supplies. Table 2 shows AS Bangi daily supplies.

Table 2   AS Bangi Daily Supplies

AS Bangi Daily Supplies	Kilograms
Fish variety	300
Squids	70
Shrimps	40
Lala	50
Petai	7
Banana leaf	5
Charcoal	50

Source: Interview with the owner of AS Bangi

To lease or to buy land

In June 2014, En. Izam learnt that the land he was renting from CDSH to operate his business might not be extended. The new Chairman of CDSH decided to build a condotel on that land. The news prompted En. Izam to search for a new business location.

In December 2014, En. Izam was offered to open a new outlet in Shah Alam by Dato' Manan, managing director of Nerusan Sdn. Bhd. (subsequently known as Nerusan). Nerusan owned a piece of land at Seksyen 13 Shah Alam. Dato' Manan was amazed with AS Bangi exotic foods when he visited Tanjung Lumpur in November 2014. He wanted En. Izam to lease Nerusan land for an extended period. New commercial and residential developments surrounded the land. Even though En. Izam learnt that other restaurateurs also highly sought the land; he submitted his proposal to Nerusan.

While waiting for the result, En. Izam still looked for another vacant land around Shah Alam. To his surprise, in late January 2015, En. Izam received a phone call from CDSH. En. Izam was informed about CDSH's intention of not pursuing the condotel project. He was relieved and quickly renewed the contract. However, the rental price had increased from RM 4,500 per month to RM6,000 per month, and the period of land lease was reduced from four years to three years, and thus, the new lease started in June 2015 and would expire in May 2018. Realising that there was no guarantee that the land lease would be extended in the future and a sharp increase of rent amount, En. Izam continued with his plan, finding a new business location.

In June 2015, En. Izam learnt that the structural organisation of Nerusan changed. Dato' Manan was no longer serving Nerusan. Without Dato' Manan in Nerusan, En. Izam felt his plan to lease the land might fail. Without internal support from Nerusan, his bid to lease land might falter because most of the bidders were established companies; meanwhile, AS Bangi performed well and gained an increase of 25 per cent in sales in 2014.

To purchase land near Bangi

In September 2015, En. Izam learned that there was vacant land for sale near the Bangi area. He was excited when he heard this news. He surveyed the area later. The land area was about

0.75 acres and located near Alamanda, Southville City, Malaysia France Institute, Kolej MARA, and Universiti Kebangsaan Malaysia. It can be accessed from PLUS South-North highway. The area can be reached through exits to Bandar Baru Bangi, Kajang, Putrajaya, Cheras, Seri Kembangan, Nilai or Kuala Lumpur from PLUS South-North highway. The area was quite near to the existing AS Bangi. The asking price of the 0.75 acres of land was RM380,000. Moreover, the land status was agricultural land. To change its status to industrial land could take some time to be approved by the Selangor Town and Country Planning department and Kajang Municipal Council. To apply for a land conversion may also cost around RM6,000 per acre. En. Izam also needed to submit the plan location and the building plan to the authorities. That would also incur some costs. It was quite a long process and involved some agencies. Thus, En. Izam must consider several things before buying the land, including the cost of putting up a new building on the land. To increase accessibility to the area, he had to improve the road condition and widened it. There were a few competitors in that area too, such as Ikan Bakar Terangkat, Perantau Hill restaurant and Medan Ikan Bakar Sungai Merab.

To lease land at Seksyen 7, Shah Alam

About the same time in September 2015, En. Izam spotted a land at Seksyen 7, Shah Alam. The land area was about a quarter acre. The land rental was around RM12,000 per month. It could be accessed from Federal and NKVE highways. The land was situated near a commercial area and had excellent market potential. It also located next to a petrol station. There were many restaurants in the area. Several competitors were already sat foot at Seksyen 7, like Ikan Bakar Maju, Restoran Arang Ikan Bakar, Mee Ketam Restaurant and Jemari Restaurant. If En. Izam wanted to buy this land, he must consider the cost to develop the land. He might need to build a new building and wait at least six months before he could start his business. In addition, En. Izam was also worried about small parking spaces available for his customers. A full-service restaurant like AS Bangi required a large parking area for its customers.

To lease shop lots at Ken Rimba, Shah Alam

In March 2016, En. Izam spotted an area at Ken Rimba, Shah Alam. Ken Rimba was located at the cities border between Klang and Shah Alam. The location could attract new customers from northern Selangor. The location also had many high-rise condos, and it was near to I-City, one of the most attractive places in Shah Alam. The easy access from the federal highway made it accessible from any direction. There were many other attractions nearby, such as Jakel, Gulatis Silk House, Hospital Shah Alam and UiTM Shah Alam. In addition, Ken Rimba had adopted the Green Building Ecosystem concept that made it a more attractive offer for the customers. The seating capacity at Ken Rimba was expected to be about

400. Despite Ken Rimba advantages, En. Izam must also consider a few other things. The rental was RM20,000 a month for two double-storey shop lots. He would also need about RM1.2 million to renovate the shop lots, purchase equipment and stock up inventories. There were a few competitors in that area, such as Arang Ikan Bakar, Muara Tanjung Harapan and Medan Port Klang. Arang Ikan Bakar, which was operationalised in 2014 and was only 2km away from Ken Rimba. Muara Tanjung Harapan was established in 2002 and located about 10km from Ken Rimba.

Moving forward

It was already the end of March 2016. En. Izam felt unsure, not knowing if what he had done so far was sufficient. He was talking to himself, "What else should I do now? The next management meeting is just around the corner. I must put together a proposal now. Shall AS Bangi purchase land near Bangi, lease land at Section 7 or rent shop lots at Ken Rimba?"

While En. Izam was thinking deeply about the possible new business location, his phone rang.

Pn. Naura:	Hello, Izam. How are you doing so far?
En. Izam:	I am about to finalise the proposal now.
Pn. Naura:	That's great. We don't want to be caught by surprise again, do we?
En. Izam:	That's right. I'll call you when it's ready.
Pn. Naura:	Ok…talk to you soon. Bye.

Acknowledgements

The authors wish to thank En. Izam Mohamed, the owner and lead entrepreneur of Ayub Seafood Bangi, for allocating a considerable amount of time and providing valuable information for this teaching case. The study was supported by Case Writing Grant, No.: R.K. 130000.7863.4L408, entitled "Growth Strategy for Ayub Seafood Bangi."

References

Agriculture and Agrifood Canada, Market Access Secretariat Global Analysis Report. (2014). Foodservice Profile Malaysia. http://www.agr.gc.ca/resources/prod/Internet- Internet/MISB-DGSIM/ATS-SEA/PDF/6519-eng.pdf. Accessed on March 31, 2017.

Cardas Research & Consulting Sdn Bhd. (2015). Food and Dining Market Malaysia Final Report.http://www.crcg.com.my/v3/wpcontent/uploads/2015/04/Food_and_Dining_Market_Malaysia_Overview_2015_Report_Final_Abstract.pdf. Accessed on March 31, 2017.

Department of Statistics Malaysia (DOSM). (2015). https://www.dosm.gov.my/v1/index. php?r=column/cthree&menu_id=cEhBV0xzWll6WTRjdkJienhoR290QT09. Accessed on March 20, 2017.

EPF. (2012). http://www.kwsp.gov.my/portal/en/about-epf/overview-of-the-epf. Accessed on April 1, 2017.

Euromonitor International. (2013). Foodservice data. http://www.euromonitor.com/consumer-foodservice. Accessed on March 31, 2017.

Euromonitor International. (2014). http://www.euromonitor.com/. Accessed on March 31, 2017.

Health Remedy. (2016). http://www.yourhealthremedy.com/medicinal-plants/petai-parkia- speciosa-health-benefits. Accessed on April 1, 2017.

HealthBenefitTimes.com. (2016). https://www.healthbenefitstimes.com/health-benefits-of-petai. Accessed on April 1, 2017.

Laporan Tinjaun Kajian Rancangan Struktur Negeri Selangor 2035. (2010). http://www.jpbdselangor.gov.my/Laporan/RSN_Selangor/laporantinjauan/B2.0_Pete mpatan.pdf. . Accessed on March 15, 2017.

Majlis Bandaraya Shah Alam (MBSA). (2017). http://www.mbsa.gov.my/enmy/infoshahalam/kenalishahalam/Pages/lokasi_demografi.aspx. Accessed on March 20, 2017.

SME Corporation Malaysia. (2011). http://www.smeinfo.com.my/index.php?option=com_ content&view=article&id=1159&Itemid=1126. Accessed on March 21, 2017.

SOCSO. (2015). http://www.perkeso.gov.my/en/about-us/profile.html. Accessed on April 1, 2017.

Terengganu Tourism. (2011). Otak-otak. http://www.tourism.terengganu.gov.my/eterengganu/index.php?option=com_content&view=article&catid=46:culinary&id=370:otak-otak&Itemid=230&lang=en. Accessed on March 15, 2017.

Terengganu Tourism. (2017). Local Delicacy & Traditional Cuisine. http://www.terengganu tourism.com/local_delicacy.htm. Accessed on March 15, 2017.

Tourism Malaysia. (2016). Keropok lekor, anyone? http://blog.tourism.gov.my/about/. Accessed on March 15, 2017.

Exhibit 1   Location search AS Bangi via google map

Exhibit 2   AS Bangi front view

Exhibit 3   Additional covered dining area for group bookings

Exhibit 4   The night at AS Bangi

Exhibit 5   Playground facilities at AS Bangi

Exhibit 6   Ample parking space
and paved at AS Bangi

Exhibit 7   Crackers and salted fish

Exhibit 8   AS BANGI hosted TV9's best in town program at Tanjung Lumpur

Exhibit 9   AS BANGI and TV9 crews after filming best in town program

Exhibit 10   Northern zone, central zone and southern zone of Shah Alam

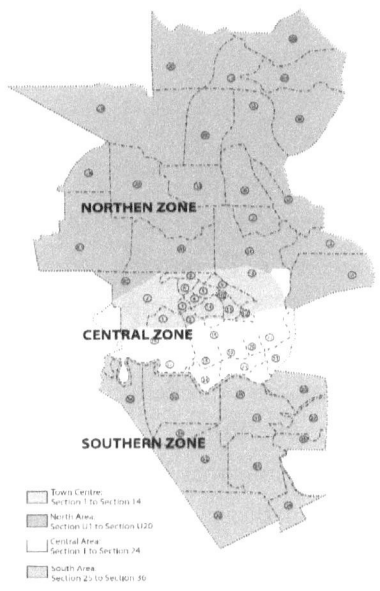

Exhibit 11   Bandar Baru Bangi map

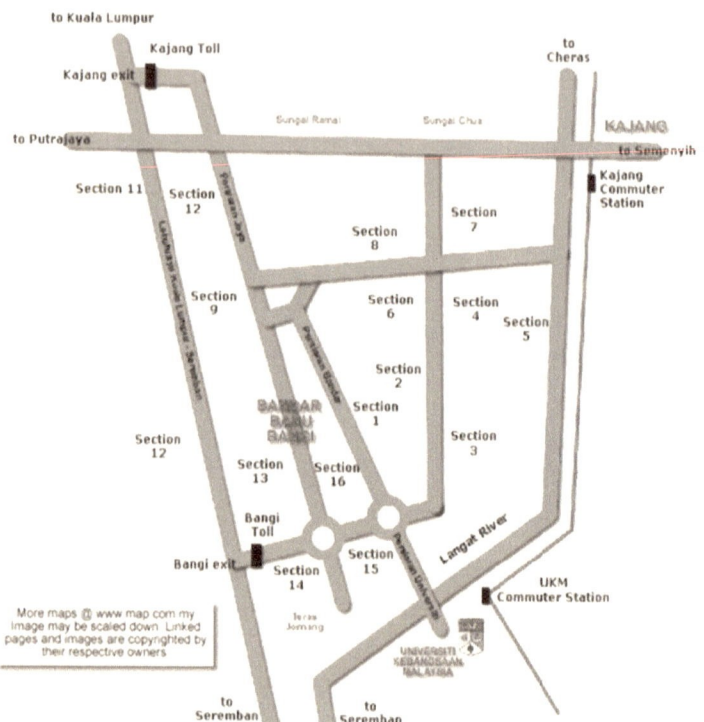

Case questions

1. Based on the teaching case of 'Ayub Seafood Bangi: Which way to go?', describe the industry and the subsector that AS Bangi operated in? What kind of products or services did AS Bangi offer?
2. Discuss the problem or dilemma faced by Ayub Seafood Bangi in March 2016?
   Explain the options that En. Izam had.
3. Conduct a situational analysis and prepare a SWOT analysis based on the information derived from the case.

4. What were the important business development milestones achieved by AS Bangi until March 2016?
5. What drove the progress of AS Bangi from one milestone to another?
6. Using the feasibility analysis, evaluate the three options that En. Izam had to choose.
7. Provide recommendation(s) to En. Izam on viable business strategy and justify your answer.

CASE #6

Street Food Concept: A Case Study On Mekcha Kopitiam

Naharudin Bin Saadan, Adriana Mohd. Rizal, Maizaitulaidawati Md Husin and Theresa Ho Char Fei

Introduction

At 3.15 pm on 1 January 2016, after meeting with the prospective franchisees at MekCha Kopitiam in Senai, Johor, Sahrom Adli, 43 (hereinafter known as the Sahrom and the founder of MekCha Kopitiam restaurants) returned to his home in Taman Scientex, Pasir Gudang. On the way home, he thought about the grievances of prospective franchisees regarding the significant increase in costs for opening new MekCha Kopitiam restaurants. Previously in 2013, the cost to open one MekCha Kopitiam restaurant was around RM 90,000 to RM 100,000. However, from mid-2015, the cost to open one MekCha Kopitiam restaurant had increased to approximately RM 150,000 to RM 200,000. Subsequently, three of the prospective franchisees had refused to continue business deals with Hex Globe Inspiration. In addition, in 2014, three of the franchisees located in Seremban, Shah Alam and

Nilai had discontinued their operations due to the increase in administrative and operating expenses. Sahrom predicted that the operational costs for MekCha Kopitiam restaurants would continue to increase by at least 25 percent after implementing the minimum wage policy (an increase of the minimum wage from RM900 to RM1200 a month) on 1 May 2016. Meanwhile, the rise in shop rentals had worsened the situation. Since 2014, rentals had increased from RM 3,000 to RM 6,000 a month and at some prime regions, the rental reached RM 10,000 a month. Sahrom began to worry as the scenario unfolded. He had to find an immediate solution because he was going to hold a MekCha Kopitiam Business Opportunity meeting with prospective franchisees on 15 April 2016 at the Johor Food Festival in Nusajaya. He was worried he would miss-out on business deals if he failed to mitigate the problem early.

Hex Globe Inspiration Sdn. Bhd. (hereinafter known as HGI) was established in 2007 and based in Pasir Gudang in Johor. HGI was set up to serve Malay food in a modern coffee restaurant setting under the brand name MekCha Kopitiam. The first restaurant opened in Kompleks Pusat Bandar Pasir Gudang in Johor. By the end of 2015, seventeen MekCha Kopitiam restaurants were operating in Johor.

In the meantime, Sahrom was reminded about the street food idea during his visit to the Street Food Business Exhibitions in Kuala Lumpur on 15 July 2014. He fell for the food truck and kiosk concept, which looked trendier, though the most important was the affordable cost. To rectify the problem, Sahrom thought of the suitability of implementing both these ideas at MekCha Kopitiam in the future.

Industry background

Approximately 25 percent (7 million of the population) of the Malaysian population experienced income growth of 1.95 percent per annum. The country had seen a steady increase in living standards with a purchasing power of RM19,700 income per capita (Statistic Department of Malaysia, 2012). According to Euromonitor (2012), this scenario had led to lifestyle changes that resulted in the demand for convenience and a simple food supply. The Malaysian food industry was greatly influenced by diverse cultures in the Malaysian society, namely the Malays, Chinese and Indians.

The Malaysian restaurant and food-service industry had seen tremendously growth. According to Euromonitor International (2012), the fast-food sector had reported a 10 percent growth in 2012, while the full-service restaurant sector experienced a 5 percent growth. Due to changing lifestyles caused by urbanization, most Malaysians rather dined out. The Malaysian Food Barometer (MFM) study found that 64 percent of Malaysians eat at least one outside meal a day (Calvin, 2014). According to a report titled "Malaysian Food Service": The future of Food Service to 2016", the profit sector accounted for 95.7 percent of total sales in 2011 with a CAGR of 3.97 percent in local currency (Canadean Ltd's, 2012). The remaining 4.3 percent of total Malaysian food service industry sales was the cost sector, which had grown at a CAGR of 2.00 percent in local currency from RM 1,769 million (USD 484 million) and RM 1,953 million (USD 640 million) in 2011.

According to Noraziah (2012), the Malaysian urban society had experienced some transformation in food consumption and eating behavior. The practice of dining-out had become a trend among urban workers, students and even families. Factors such as a working wife, working place being far from house and the preference of convenience had encouraged the practice of dining out. In the urban centre, the food business was operated either formally or informally. Usually, their presence in the crowded city ensured easy access for customers. Formal food premises operated by franchised cafes and restaurants such as KFC, McDonalds, Pizza Hut, etc. were owned by locals or foreign entrepreneurs. Normally, formal food services operated in either shop lots developed by local authorities, in food courts developed by shopping malls or in private buildings owned by individual food operators. Meanwhile, the informal food operators normally operated in smaller food premises developed by local authorities. Usually, informal food operators offered local dishes at lower prices. In the meantime, there were also mobile units and street food businesses such as hawkers, food trucks and car booth sales that operated at unauthorized spots, as they could not obtain licenses. Figure 1 shows the food pattern of daily operations.

Operation patterns	Meal types	Description of food
Single session (3 – 5 hours):		
1. Morning only	Breakfast	Nasi lemak, roti canai, noodles and local sweets, cakes
2. Afternoon only	Lunch	Rice & varieties of dishes
3. Late afternoon	Tea	Local cakes, sweets
4. Night only	Dinner, supper	Rice and accompanied dishes & ala carte
Multiple session:		
1. Morning & afternoon	Breakfast & lunch	Local dishes
2. Morning till night (10 hours)	Breakfast, lunch & dinner	Local, thais, Indians and Western*
3. Morning till the next early morning (15 hours)	Breakfast, lunch, tea, dinner & supper	Local, thais, Indians and Western
4. Afternoon till midnight (10 hours)	Lunch, dinner & supper	Local, thais, Indians and Western
5. Late afternoon till early morning (10 hours)	Tea, dinner & supper	Local, thais, Indians and Western
23 or 24 hours a day	All meals	All kinds

* Franchaise restaurants Pizza Huts, KFC, MacDonald – western only

Source from: Norazizah (2012)

Figure 1: Food pattern of daily operations

Noraziah (2012) found that dining patterns were influenced by the eatery's location, mealtimes, food types, and the eateries itself. In addition, eating behaviour was related to needs and it determines the patterns of mealtime, i.e., breakfast, lunch, and dinner. In traditional practice, the women would cook for the household and meals were served at home. However, the eating patterns had changed due to social transformation, vis-a vis urbanization.

According to the United Nations, urbanization had caused a rise in the number of street food entrepreneurs, particularly in capital cities worldwide (Food and Agriculture Organization, 2015). The demand for ready to eat food had increased as people; especially employed women, who had less time to prepare meals. The street food concept was described as a wide of range of ready-to-eat meals and drinks. The street food concept involved food being prepared in the public place, notably along the streets. Like fast food, street food preparation occurred when the customer made an order, which was normally on a take-away basis. Street food was often described as traditional local culture because most street food businesses were owned and operated by individuals or families. However, the benefits from their trade extend throughout the local economy.

The numbers of the population in Johor were expected to increase two-fold from the year 2000 to 2020 (Iskandar Malaysia Development, 2015 - refer to Appendix 1). As a capital city, Johor Bahru would have more than two million population followed by another district like Batu Pahat, Muar, and Kluang. More than 80 per cent of the total Johor population lived in these four main districts. Since the year 2010, many mega projects like Pembangunan Wilayah Iskandar, in Johor Bahru and Rapid Pengerang, in Kota Tinggi contributed to the increment in the population. Thus, the increased population would positively impact the daily need for business like food and beverages. Meanwhile, based on age, 80 percent of the population was less than 45. This range of age indicated Johor as a productive state, and the people had the purchasing power in the economy.

Company background

Sahrom, 43, obtained his bachelor's degree in Mineral Resources Engineering from Universiti Sains Malaysia. However, his interest was in the culinary and food management sector instead of the engineering field. In 1990, after he finished his tertiary education, Sahrom intended to pursue his studies in hotel management and catering. However, he had to cancel his intention, as his mother wanted him to further his studies in the engineering field. Nevertheless, his passion for the food business was nurtured since childhood. Since the age of seven, Sahrom was exposed to the food business as he assisted his parents selling food at the night market in Kluang, Johor. After graduating in 1996, he started his career as a Quality Controller (QC) at Hitachi Chemical in Pasir Gudang until 2007. As a QC, his primary task was to ensure that the quality of products manufactured met the standards adopted by the management. Besides, he was also directly involved in preparing the standard operating procedures (SOPs) based on quality philosophies such as Total Quality Management (TQM), Just in Time and 5's.

He then joined the MLM business from 2002 until 2004. In the June 2003, he managed to achieve the second highest ranking in sales achievement with the average income of RM 10,000 a month. However, Sahrom felt the MLM business was not truly a business; it was just like an intermediary who promoted and sold others' product. So finally, in May 2004, he left the MLM business to start a bakery shop business.

In September 2004, Sahrom started the bakery shop business as a Season Bakery and Confectionery franchisee at Bandar Baru UDA, Johor Bahru. He started the business with an initial capital of RM 130,000.00 which covered the franchise fee and shop renovation. Besides taking a personal financing loan with the bank, he used his entire savings to cover the outstanding amount. From 2004 to 2007, Sahrom worked at Hitachi Chemical; thus, his employees handled the operations of the bakery shop. Nevertheless, every day after work he would visit the bakery shop to check the daily operation of the business. As a franchise business, the franchisor had fixed the profit margin, so Sahrom only earned thirty-five percent of the gross margins from the total sales. With various restrictions from the franchisor, Sahrom felt demotivated to continue the bakery shop business. As a franchisee, he could not modify the existing products or services because it was not allowed by the franchisor. In the middle of April 2007, he was in the dilemma of continuing or stopping the bakery shop business. He had to pay RM 80,000 to renew the franchise fee for the next five years. Finally, in May 2007, he decided not to renew the franchise fee and closed the bakery shop business. He gained valuable experience operating the bakery business regarding the modern eatery concepts, professional staff training, and professional business management systems.

The modern coffee shop concept

The idea of a modern coffee shop came to his mind when he and his family were having dinner on 15 July 2007 in Pasir Gudang, Johor. They wanted to have original Malay delicacies like *lempeng, asam pedas, ubi rebus* etc. At that time, he found that restaurants and hawkers were mostly selling Thai food. He then realized the opportunity to setup a modern coffee shop that served Malay cuisine. He listed more than one hundred Malay cuisine menus, which he obtained from the internet and his parents, relatives, and friends. Besides that, he visited more than sixty coffee shops located in Johor to taste the variety of coffee and other menus. He noticed that the unique taste of coffee came from the technique of brewing the coffee. Therefore, he was not shy to enquire from coffee shop workers regarding the technique and method of preparing coffee and other menus. Finally, in November 2007, Sahrom succeeded in establishing his signature menu and coffee, which would later be offered in MekCha Kopitiam. In the early stages of the establishment, MekCha Kopitiam only offered basic meals such as *roti bakar kahwin MekCha, ubi rebus, bihun goreng MekCha, kueh tiow goreng MekCha, kopi O MekCha* and *kopi MekCha*. By the end of 2015, there were over fifty food and beverage menus under the brand name of MekCha Kopitiam.

The name 'MekCha' was chosen in conjunction with the historic name of the place where his parents got married, the name of a small village located in Kluang, Johor. While the word of 'kopitiam' is a Malay/ Hokkien term referring to a traditional coffee shop found mostly in Southeast Asia and patronized for meals and beverages. Besides the unique signature menu, Sahrom noticed that the attraction of a modern coffee shop came from the unique interior design and professional business management system. Then in November 2007, he faced capital constraints in starting his business; he only had RM 60,000 to do the renovation, buy the equipment and pay for other start-up business expenses. Due to capital constraints, he used "Pallet Wood" for the floors and counters, which he obtained from Hitachi Chemical free of charge. In mid-2015, he realized that he was the pioneer in using "Pallet Wood" as a unique raw material in coffee shop construction.

For future expansion, he realized that the business had to be managed by a private limited company. Hence, in November 2007 he bought an already existing company called Hex Globe Inspiration Sdn. Bhd. from the company secretary with Sahrom and his brother, Saiful Bahri Adli, becoming directors of the company. He was appointed as Managing Director. In December 2007, the first MekCha Kopitiam restaurant opened in Kompleks Pusat Bandar Pasir Gudang in Johor. On the first day of operations, MekCha Kopitiam managed to achieve sales of RM570.00. The sales trend increased from day to day until it reached RM 2000.00 to RM 2500.00 in May 2008. After operating for three months, in February 2008 he left Hitachi Chemical to concentrate on MekCha Kopitiam fully.

Success Formula of MekCha Kopitiam

Sahrom believed that maintaining the unique taste of recipes, besides the quality of the service, was the key success factor in the MekCha Kopitiam episode. Therefore, he had to ensure that every employee played an important role, either at the kitchen or at the customer service section. He noticed that employee turnover was a common problem faced by every eatery business.

The common practice was that most of the employees at the eatery only wanted to work temporarily and would leave when they found a better job. Thus, over-dependence on employees could damage the business as the owner frequently needed to find and train new employees when the position became vacant. Hence, he thought the problems could be solved by establishing a standard operating procedure for each process in the MekCha Kopitiam restaurant. He then created written standards known as MekCha SOP for each work process for each food recipe offered by MekCha Kopitiam. Moreover, to maintain the standard taste of each recipe in all MekCha Kopitiam restaurants, he had fixed special cooking equipment. The custom- made culinary equipment allowed the employee to measure the ingredient accurately for each menu based on these standards. By instilling these standards, Sahrom was able to train new employees within three day and mitigate the risk of losing employees. Subsequently, each MekCha Kopitiam restaurant managed to achieve the sixty percent gross profit target for their businesses.

Sahrom also adopted the cash management system (CMS) at MekCha Kopitiam restaurant since commencing the business in 2007. The CMS was an integrated system that linked sales with the customer ordering system. He put lots of effort into introducing the information system at each MekCha Kopitiam outlet. Sahrom believed the IT support system would increase efficiency in managing resources and productivity in the MekCha Kopitiam outlet. Every MekCha Kopitiam outlet needed to use the CMS to manage daily cash flow transactions. The customers could use different kinds of payment transactions like cash, credit card, and debit card. Besides, the CMS was integrated with the table order number and menu prepared by the staffs' kitchen. The ordering process in MekCha started with customers ordering the food from the menu in the catalog and written them in order notes. Then, the waiter keyed in the menu on the device, which simultaneously updated the order at the kitchen department. When the kitchen staff saw the customer orders from the order screen, they prepared the menus using the first in, first-out (FIFO) concept. Once the food was ready, the kitchen staff notified the waiter to send the dish to the respective tables. After the order was sent to the customer, the waiter updated the cashier. Finally, the customer needed to inform their table number to pay their food before leaving the restaurant. As such, MekCha Kopitiam was able to minimize the mishandling of cash among employees.

Sahrom also created a commission-based policy in MekCha Kopitiam. The commission policy was based on the daily sales target. If the sales of MekCha Kopitiam outlet achieved the daily sales target, every staff would entitle to a commission as a reward. As a result, the employee was eager to promote and pull the customer to MekCha Kopitiam outlets. Sahrom felt the policy had successfully contributed to employees' entrepreneurial mindsets, loyalty, teamwork, and reduced employee turnover in MekCha Kopitiam. According to Sahrom, some former employees returned to MekCha Kopitiam after leaving the business due to the team's good spirit adopted in MekCha Kopitiam. Sahrom also tried to resolve any problem arose to ensure overall productivity of the company.

Through the cash management system, MekCha Kopitiam outlets could pinpoint the popular menus ordered by their customers. The system also gathered information on sales trends, profitability, and outlet performance. According to En Sahrom, each MekCha Kopitiam franchise could forecast the demand of its customers, such as the types of food preferred by their customers and when they chose to have them. As such, the data gave them a head start and let them gain a competitive advantage compared to other eatery businesses. In addition, the data helped the company manage its stock and ensured there would be enough raw materials to prepare the popular dishes in MekCha Kopitiam. By following a proper business plan, MekCha Kopitiam managed to obtain a breakeven point in one and half year with an annual growth rate of eight percent.

MekCha Kopitiam as a franchise brand

Initially, Sahrom never thought of turning MekCha Kopitiam into a franchise brand. However, upon requests from loyal customers, he finally agreed to register MekCha Kopitiam as a franchise brand in 2013. Since the franchise-license application process took a long time, so in 2009 he started with the licensing contract due to interested parties eagerly wanted to operate a MekCha Kopitiam. He realized the importance of brand protection and applied for the franchise license, which he finally obtained on 5 December 2013. MekCha Kopitiam was officially registered as a franchise brand under the Ministry of Domestic Trade and Consumer Affairs of Malaysia on that date. Under the MekCha Kopitiam franchise, the franchisee would enjoy the training program consisting of restaurant management systems, raw materials, restaurant equipment, and employee training. As a franchise holder, Hex Globe Inspiration (HGI) would earn a franchise fee of RM 40,000 for a five-year contract and royalties from restaurant sales of four percent. Besides that, HGI would become the sole supplier of raw materials for the food and beverages offered at each MekCha Kopitiam restaurant.

Right until the end of 2015, seventeen coffee restaurants were operating under the MekCha Kopitiam brand.

Financial performance

Based on the Sales Report (refer to Appendix 5) from 2013 until 2015, HGI sales steadily grew at 25 percent per annum. 60 percent of the revenue derived from the sale of the raw material, while 32 percent was from direct outlet sales and the remaining 7 percent from sales royalty. The sale of the raw material was the main income for HGI. This segment was generated RM2.70 million in 2015, RM1.90 million in 2014 and RM1.70 million in 2013.

In 2015, the total sales for 17 MekCha Kopitiam restaurants reached RM7.70 million (refer to Appendix 2). The amount was expected to increase in 2016 due to the increase in new MekCha Kopitiam outlets. Six of the outlets had recorded sales of more than RM0.5 million, with MekCha Gelang Patah had recorded the highest sales with RM1.12 million. In addition, MekCha Angsana Johor Bahru recorded RM0.82 million sales, MekCha Pasir Gudang recorded RM0.67 million sales, MekCha Taman Perling recorded RM0.62 million sales, MekCha Leisure Mall recorded RM0.54 million sales and MekCha Johor Port recorded RM0.52 million sales respectively.

Roughly, HGI had secured 35 percent by selling raw material at each MekCha outlet (refer to Appendix 3) Although this segment was the main contributor to HGI turnover, HGI only gained 19 percent profit from this segment. Based on the contract, the MekCha outlets were required to buy raw materials from HGI. As a result, HGI spent 81 percent in the cost of sales in producing the raw material.

HGI also generated income from direct sales from its MekCha outlet. As a result, the total revenue was steadily increased from 2013 until 2015. In 2015, this segment was recorded about RM1.44 million sales. HGI owned three outlets in MekCha Pasir Gudang, MekCha Kotaraya, and MekCha Mersing. MekCha Pasir Gudang recorded the highest sales among the three outlets in 2015 with total sales of RM0.68 million, followed by MekCha Kota Raya with RM0.48 million and MekCha Mersing of RM0.27 million (refer to Appendix 2). As such, HGI was able to secure at least 55 percent of gross profit from this segment. Sahrom believed that by having proper management in MekCha outlets, the revenues from this segment would continue to sustain in next coming year.

The HGI's turnover also was generated from sales royalty. Based on the contract, HGI earned a 4 percent of the royalty fee from MekCha outlet sales. On average, HGI gained RM18 thousand for each MekCha outlet, with a total income of RM308 thousand a year (see Appendix 4). The royalty income was a passive income, but for HGI, the fee was the trust money acquired from its franchisee. HGI had to continue to build the MekCha Kopitiam brand for the benefit of its franchisee. Sahrom had prioritized research and development to sustain the MekCha Kopitiam brand in the market. Each year, HGI allocated thirty percent of its annual budget for R&D activities. Previously, R&D activities had focused on searching for new menus and recipes. However, future R&D activities would involve the restaurant concept, trends, and designs as key areas of attention. Given that the operational and administrative expenses were around 50 percent, HGI had succeeded in generating a total net profit of RM850,000.

Case closure

The increase in property prices had caused many food entrepreneurs to use various methods to promote, sell and distribute their products. Sahrom had thought about a way to assist prospective franchisees to overcome the substantial cost incurred when opening a new MekCha Kopitiam. He anticipated that by mid-2016, the food truck business would become a trend in Johor Bahru. Thus, he thought of naming the food truck business concept as "MekCha on Wheels" (refer to Appendix 6), a practical idea intended to assist prospective franchisees. In the meantime, the "MekCha Kiosk" (refer to Appendix 6) concept was also given due consideration. The increasing number of shopping malls in Johor Bahru was an opportunity for MekCha Kopitiam to market and distribute its products. Both options would require 2 to 3 employees with a total estimated salary of RM 4,000 per month. However, the rental cost for MekCha Kiosk was slightly higher compared to "MekCha on Wheels".

The Food truck concept

The cost of starting a food truck business was lower and the process was faster than opening a restaurant. The lower expenses factor made the food truck business the best avenue for first time food entrepreneurs. They would be able to learn the landscape while providing invaluable experience that was beneficial for future undertakings. Moreover, food trucks could also compliment the catering business by expanding their market without drastic changes in operations. The food truck business was going to be much more fascinating compared to restaurants. Providing the takeaway concept would create an opportunity for people to enjoy food in a bustling working environment. In the meantime, working on a food truck would rarely be bored because the service would be faster and more enjoyable as business owners developed rapport with customers when they became regulars. Depending on the size, brand and equipment, starting a food truck business would range from RM 60,000 to RM 70,000. However, the cost could be reduced if a second-hand truck was used. However, the challenge for the food truck sector was the regulation and by-laws. Until 2015, the local authorities had yet to finalize the regulations and by-laws regarding the food truck business. There would be a possibility that the restaurant business circle might lobby the regulator against endorsing the food truck business due to increasing competition and uncertain regulations. This would make starting a food truck business even more challenging.

The food kiosk concept

The food kiosk concept would be typically good for serving simple food like sandwiches, donuts, cupcakes, and other small meals that would not require heated (refer to Appendix 7). Coffee, tea, and other soft drinks were also suitable for the food kiosk. However, cooking in a kiosk required a ventilation system to ensure smoke and odors would not enter the indoor facility. For this reason, the food kiosk would be suitable for operation in food courts where both ventilation and electricity were available. The costs involved in opening a food kiosk would range from RM 30,000 to RM 50,000 depending on the size and design. Generally, the food kiosk would be suitable for operating in shopping malls, bus stations, hotels, airports, and amusement parks. However, the rental would be higher if the kiosk would be operating in a busy location.

Sahrom felt that it was time for MekCha Kopitiam to diversify its business model. However, he was worried as to whether prospective franchisees and customers would accept his idea. Besides, he also thought about the suitable menus and recipes for the new business concept. Lastly, he knew the advantage of being a first mover; he felt that he had to react promptly and not miss-out on the opportunities.

References

Calvin, T. (2014, August 3). More Malaysians eat out nowadays but are we eating enough healthy food? *The Star*. https://www.thestar.com.my/news/nation/2014/08/03/food- always-on-our-minds-more-malaysians-eat-out-nowadays-but-are-we-eating-enough- healthy-food/

Canadean Ltd. (2012, August). *Research and Markets: Malaysian Foodservice: The Future of Foodservice to 2016.* http://www.researchandmarkets.com/research/z55kmr/malaysian foodserve

Department of Statistics of Malaysia. (2012). Household Expenditure Survey 2009–2010

(MYS_2009_HES_v01_M). https://catalog.ihsn.org/index.php/catalog/5430

Euromonitor International. (2012). *Fast food in Malaysia*. https://www.euromonitor.com/fast- food-in-malaysia/report

Food and Agriculture Organization. (2015, April). *FOOD IN AN URBANISED WORLD The Role of City Region Food Systems in Resilience and Sustainable Development*. fao.org. http://www.fao.org/fileadmin/templates/agphome/documents/horticulture/crfs/foodurbani zed.pdf

Johor State Investment Centre. Johor's Population. (2015). Iskandar Malaysia Development. http://www.iskandarmalaysia.com.my/why-invest-in-iskandar-malaysia

Noraziah, A. (2012). The food consumption and eating behaviour of Malaysian urbanites: Issues and concerns. *The Food Consumption and Eating Behaviour of Malaysian Urbanites: Issues and Concerns*, 8(Issue 6 (157–165)), 157–165. https://ejournal.ukm.my/

Exhibit 1

Johor's Population, 2000-2020

District	2000	2005	2010	1015	2020
Johor Bahru	1,159,079	1,370,738	1,613,221	1,880,729	2,170,423
Batu Pahat	353,129	382,175	412,469	440,559	466,106
Muar	348,662	373,587	398,766	421,189	441,024
Kluang	272,161	295,373	319,629	342,193	363,270
Kota Tinggi	199,024	212,558	226,104	238,130	248,311
Segamat	188,968	198,142	206,577	213,443	218,213
Pontian	149,647	160,722	171,291	180,781	189,369
Mersing	69,947	73,920	77,766	80,896	83,606
Total	2,740,617	3,067,215	3,425,823	3,797,920	4,180,322

Age group of population in Johor

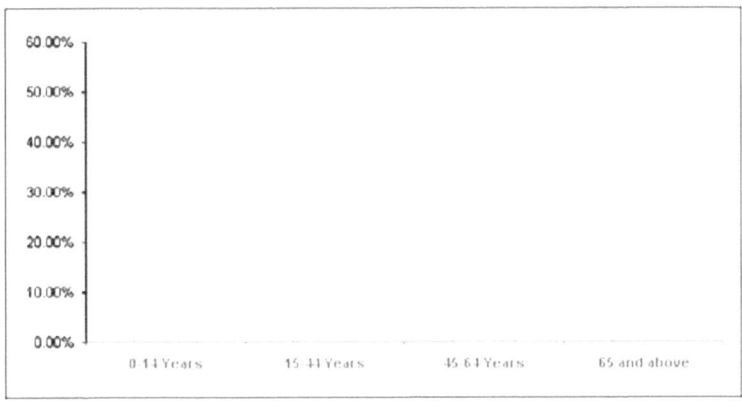

Exhibit 2 Total MekCha kopitiam turnover in 2015

Outlet	CO/FO	Jan-15 RM	Feb-15 RM	Mar-15 RM	Apr-15 RM	May-15 RM	Jun-15 RM	Jul-15 RM	Aug-15 RM	Sep-15 RM	Oct-15 RM	Nov-15 RM	Dec-15 RM	Total (RM)
P.Gudang	CO	64,423.36	54,804.25	59,893.60	64,659.60	69,445.20	41,733.35	26,401.45	71,406.20	56,595.88	55,617.44	55,719.09	55,197.28	675,896.69
Leisure Mall	FO	45,894.85	43,323.31	47,850.00	48,900.00	49,780.00	35,670.00	40,650.00	51,360.00	45,428.52	45,370.23	45,626.09	45,348.11	545,201.11
Bdr Baru Uda	FO	45,624.00	37,204.00	41,318.00	36,597.00	39,281.00	25,386.00	29,877.00	35,491.00	36,347.25	35,187.66	34,935.61	34,137.81	431,386.33
Perling	FO	59,318.00	53,710.00	64,152.00	59,675.00	61,960.00	41,414.00	21,632.00	57,035.00	52,362.00	51,492.50	51,215.31	49,598.23	623,564.04
Danga Bay	FO	19,424.30	15,377.00	19,833.20	17,525.40	20,465.00	22,980.00	15,760.00	23,154.00	19,314.86	19,301.18	19,791.71	19,786.52	232,713.17
Angsana	FO	27,402.00	41,665.00	61,013.00	64,604.00	75,320.00	90,870.00	97,200.00	75,470.00	66,693.00	71,604.38	75,346.80	77,138.52	824,326.69
Bandar Penawar	FO	36,423.00	33,811.00	33,835.00	28,631.15	37,690.00	24,800.00	21,600.00	40,250.00	32,130.02	31,593.40	31,316.20	31,001.35	383,081.11
Setia Tropika	FO	46,906.00	35,002.00	43,813.00	36,572.00	45,670.00		12,497.00	41,309.00	32,721.13	30,948.02	30,441.27	28,769.80	384,649.21
Tmn Universiti	FO	20,720.77	21,983.61	23,993.00	23,508.00	24,736.00	16,490.00	9,621.00	20,817.00	20,233.67	20,172.79	19,946.43	19,440.61	241,662.88
Taman Daya	FO	29,398.00	27,846.00	26,390.00	24,322.00	24,916.00	19,375.00	12,194.00	20,942.00	23,172.88	22,394.73	21,713.33	21,128.74	273,792.68
Kota Masai	FO	34,616.00	28,704.00	29,295.00	25,646.00	24,236.00	17,133.00	16,482.00	19,557.00	24,458.63	23,188.95	22,499.57	21,650.14	287,466.29
Kotaraya	CO	52,267.00	44,104.00	52,131.28	41,812.00	41,711.00	31,498.00	25,463.00	33,816.00	40,350.29	38,860.70	38,205.28	36,464.53	476,683.08
Mersing	CO	20,121.20	24,957.10	24,109.40	22,487.30	25,172.90	19,645.70	14,691.00	25,600.00	22,098.08	22,345.18	22,018.69	21,757.36	265,003.91
Gelang Patah	FO	101,160.00	98,497.00	110,363.00	108,386.00	103,491.00	73,705.00	73,797.00	79,048.00	93,555.88	92,605.36	91,868.90	89,557.14	1,116,034.28
Senai	FO								42,386.00	43,657.58	44,967.31	46,316.33	47,705.82	225,033.03
Johor Port	FO	46,737.15	44,211.00	45,318.25	45,094.80	46,170.40	40,107.10	40,096.00	45,704.90	44,179.95	43,860.30	43,816.46	43,628.74	528,925.05
Kota Kinabalu	FO								35,451.00	36,514.53	37,609.97	38,738.26	39,900.41	188,214.17
Total		650,435.63	605,199.27	683,307.73	648,420.25	690,044.50	500,807.15	457,961.45	718,797.10	689,814.12	687,120.08	689,515.34	682,211.11	7,703,633.73

CO TURNOVER

OUTLETS	AMOUNT (RM)
P.Gudang	675,896.69
Bandar Penawar	383,081.11
Setia Tropika	384,649.21
TOTAL	**1,443,627.01**

Note:
- CO - COMPANY OWNER
- FO - FRANCHISE OWNER

Exhibit 3 Sales on raw material consumption in 2015 of Hex Globe Inpiration Sdn Bhd

No.	Outlet	Co/fo	Total outlet sales	Sales on material Consumption	Cost of sales	Gross profit	Profit
1	P.Gudang	CO	675,896.69	236,563.84	191,616.71	44,947.13	19%
2	Leisure Mall	FO	545,201.11	190,820.39	154,564.51	36,255.87	19%
3	Bdr Baru Uda	FO	431,386.33	150,985.22	122,298.03	28,687.19	19%
4	Perling	FO	623,564.04	218,247.41	176,780.41	41,467.01	19%
5	Danga Bay	FO	232,713.17	81,449.61	65,974.18	15,475.43	19%
6	Angsana	FO	824,326.69	288,514.34	233,696.62	54,817.73	19%
7	Bandar Penawar	FO	383,081.11	134,078.39	108,603.49	25,474.89	19%
8	Setia Tropika	FO	384,649.21	134,627.22	109,048.05	25,579.17	19%
9	Tmn Universiti	FO	241,662.88	84,582.01	68,511.43	16,070.58	19%
10	Taman Daya	FO	273,792.68	95,827.44	77,620.22	18,207.21	19%
11	Kota Masai	FO	287,466.29	100,613.20	81,496.69	19,116.51	19%
12	Kotaraya	CO	476,683.08	166,839.08	135,139.65	31,699.42	19%
13	Mersing	CO	265,003.91	92,751.37	75,128.61	17,622.76	19%
14	Gelang Patah	FO	1,116,034.28	390,612.00	316,395.72	74,216.28	19%
15	Senai	FO	225,033.03	78,761.56	63,796.86	14,964.70	19%
16	Johor Port	FO	528,925.05	185,123.77	149,950.25	35,173.52	19%
17	Kota Kinabalu	FO	188,214.17	65,874.96	53,358.72	12,516.24	19%
TOTAL			7,703,633.73	2,696,271.80	2,183,980.16	512,291.64	19%

Notes:
- CO - COMPANY OWNER
- FO - FRANCHISE OWNER

Exhibit 4 MekCha kopitiam sales royalty in 2015

NO.	OUTLET	CO/FO	TOTAL OUTLET SALES	ROYALTY FEE
1	P.Gudang	CO	675,896.69	27,035.87
2	Leisure Mall	FO	545,201.11	21,808.04
3	Bdr Baru Uda	FO	431,386.33	17,255.45
4	Perling	FO	623,564.04	24,942.56
5	Danga Bay	FO	232,713.17	9,308.53
6	Angsana	FO	824,326.69	32,973.07
7	Bandar Penawar	FO	383,081.11	15,323.24
8	Setia Tropika	FO	384,649.21	15,385.97
9	Tmn Universiti	FO	241,662.88	9,666.52
10	Taman Daya	FO	273,792.68	10,951.71
11	Kota Masai	FO	287,466.29	11,498.65
12	Kotaraya	CO	476,683.08	19,067.32
13	Mersing	CO	265,003.91	10,600.16
14	Gelang Patah	FO	1,116,034.28	44,641.37
15	Senai	FO	225,033.03	9,001.32
16	Johor Port	FO	528,925.05	21,157.00
17	Kota Kinabalu	FO	188,214.17	7,528.57
	TOTAL		7,703,633.73	308,145.35

Notes:
- CO - COMPANY OWNER
- FO - FRANCHISE OWNER

Exhibit 5   Hex Globe Inspiration Sdn Bhd turnover from 2013 – 2015 (In millions RM)

Year	Raw Material Sales	Direct Own Sales	Sales Royalty	Total Sales
2015	2,696,271.80	1,443,627.01	308,145.35	4,448,044.16
2014	1,925,136.00	1,374,882.86	235,987.00	3,536,005.86
2013	1,698,579.00	1,309,412.25	215,398.00	3,223,389.25

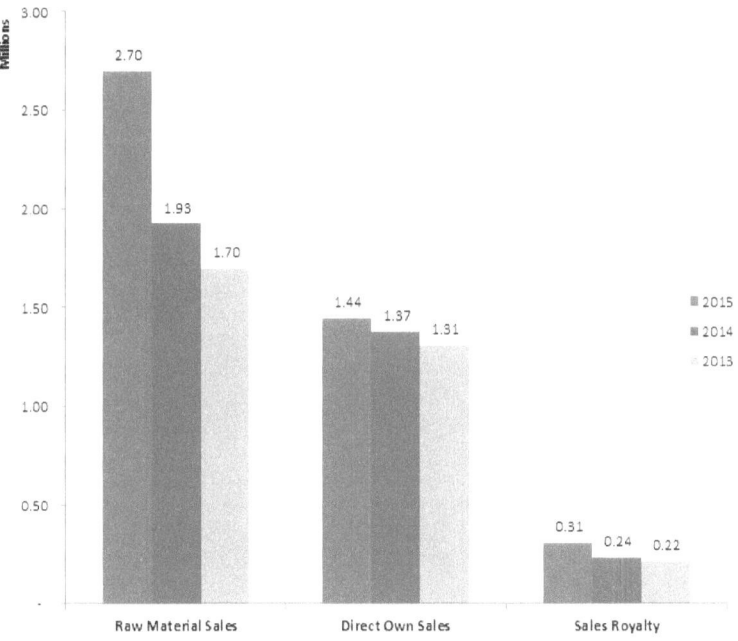

Exhibit 6   MekCha on wheel and MekCha kiosk

Exhibit 7 The proposal menus for MekCha on wheel and MekCha kiosk

a. Breakfast (7.30 am - 11.00 am)

No	Food	Drink
1	MekCha Sandwich	Kopi O MekCha
2	MekCha Roti Kawin	Kopi Susu MekCha
3	Nasi Lemak MekCha	The Tarik MekCha
4	Lempeng MekCha	Bancau MekCha
5	Ubi Rebus MekCha	Cappucino MekCha

b. Lunch (12.00 pm - 3.00pm)

No	Food	Drink
1	Nasi Goreng MekCha	Kopi O MekCha
2	Mee Goreng MekCha	Kopi Susu MekCha
3		The Tarik MekCha
4		Bancau MekCha
5		Cappucino MekCha

c. Dinner (5.30 pm - 10.00 pm)

No	Food	Drink
1	Nasi Paprik MekCha	Kopi O MekCha
2	Nasi Ayam MekCha	Kopi Susu MekCha
3	Nasi Goreng MekCha	The Tarik MekCha
4	Mee Goreng MekCha	Bancau MekCha
5		Cappucino MekCha

Case questions

1. What personal attributes possessed by Sahrom as a successful entrepreneur?
2. When did Sahrom realizes that he needed to diversify the business channel distribution for the new MekCha Kopitiam franchisee?
3. Conduct the analysis for both options according to marketing mix analysis (4P's)?
4. What are the challenges faced by Sahrom in promoting MekCha on Wheel and MekCha Kiosk?
5. What would you recommend Sahrom to do? Justify your answers.

CASE #7

Nextra: Inefficiency in Managing Cleaning Service Contractor

Sare Yasseen Iderosee, Nor Aiza Mohd Zamil and Siti Zaleha Abdul Rasid

Introduction

Although the Tripartite Agreement looks great on paper with proper documentation and workflow, the reality is not as agreed in the agreement. Ms Rini felt that NEXTRA Co. (M) Bhd. (NEXTRA) position as the client does not benefit them in terms of cost and service performance. Ms Rini has been receiving many complaints from Housekeeping Supervisor. Also, it is reported that there is an increased number of customers complaints related to NEXTRA cleanliness, such as cleaner attitude problem, late delivery of hygiene and consumable items including tissue and foam soap, and poor quality of products supplied such as floor mat that causing hazard to customers.

"Although I have tried to resolve every issue reported, things get complicated as I need to discuss with the mediator, Nextra Choice Malaysia (NCM) before the issue can be reported to the service provider." Ms Rini mumbled to herself. The Tripartite Agreement has caused a communication breakdown between NEXTRA and Malaysia Cleaning (MC). Sometimes, the issue reported to NCM may not be appropriately delivered to MC due to the understanding gap and many issues that required a longer time to resolve. The worst-case scenario is when problems are left unattended with all of the issues and topics reported by NEXTRA outlets, coupled with poor cooperation from NCM and MC. Things get more complicated when Mr Asahi announced in the Board meeting that the new direction for the company is "Back to Basic" and directed Internal Auditor (IA) to audit the Housekeeping department. "And now the IA's personnel is questioning me regarding the monitoring and compliance to payment processes, lack of proper procedure in place and inconsistency of documentation in Requisition and Proposal (R&P) flow."

The retail industry

The retail industry has become one of the commercial sectors that contributed to Malaysia's GDP and served the employment industry for employees around the nation. Its dynamic factor has to make the industry very competitive in driving sales and getting profit, and ensuring customer's acceptance to stay loyal to the retailers. However, in recent years, the instabilities of Malaysia currency has been seen, especially after the crumpling of oil price in 2015, affecting Malaysia economic position that heavily depends on oil exports for its governmental revenue. In April 2015, 6% GST was implemented to increase national revenues and reduce the shortfalls. With all the economic challenges and struggles, most industries in Malaysia are upset, including the retail sector. Furthermore, 2016 witnessed a substantial drop in retail industry growth where the rate was 95% below approximation made by Malaysia Retails Association (MRA) (at 5.5%).

Despite all the challenges, in 2016, the retail industry is recovering from its fall. The industry sales grew at 1.7% compared to only 1.4% in 2015. However, the MRA members have forecast the growth rate of sales performance in Malaysia for the first quarter of 2017 to increase only 0.9% due to consumers' sentiment, where the rising cost of living has impacted the purchasing power of Malaysian consumers. Retailers need more than just attractive goods to give added value to the customers.

In 2018, Malaysia's overall retail sales were expected to accomplish higher sales performance with a progress of 6% compared to 3.7% in the 2017 year's growth. An increment of the sales performance is expected to be influenced by several factors, including the forthcoming general election (GE) in Malaysia that could help to improve the percentage of earlier prediction of a 5% increase. If the election takes place before the middle of the year, there is an anticipated that there would be an increase in growth in the retail industry economy. It is believed that once the election is over, consumers' confidence is going to boost and stimulate economic growth and performance. Besides GE, the ringgit forecast to a stable level by the end of next year would influence the economic growth and is expected to boost the overall retail sales. However, the industry remains hopeful that when the currency exchange rate returns to where it was in 2014, the cost of living will be reduced to a more comfortable and affordable level and increase the purchasing power of the people.

Besides consumers are being priced sensitive, the industry had been forced to cope with the price rising in the cost of goods sold, which affected the cost of most items. Furthermore, the volatility of Malaysia currency affected NEXTRA operations to maintain the competitive price, especially for goods imported from other countries. However, in NEXTRA, competitive prices and the quality of goods sold have been one of their solid advantages for over 30 years. NEXTRA also focuses on its customer service and aim to provide an excellent shopping experience to its customers parallel with their tagline, "Enriching Your Lifestyles".

The housekeeping department

To enhance competitive ability in the industry, a retail company should compete among competitors with excellent and valuable merchandise selection and ensure customer satisfaction and loyalty. It is proven that companies that are successful in keeping loyal customers would have a greater competitive advantage. Hygiene and cleanliness could be factors that resulted in customer loyalty because they will provide a tremendous and enjoyable customers shopping experience. In NEXTRA, the cleanliness of the store is being monitored by Headquarter (HQ) Housekeeping Department. This department consists of two personnel who are holding the position of manager and officer. Both are responsible for managing overall housekeeping activity for the whole NEXTRA company.

Before 2015, the payment to cleaning services providers was made by the outlets that rendered their services. However, in 2015, the General Manager (GM), Mr Ahmad, decided to centralize all payments to HQ Housekeeping Department.

The initiative was introduced to reduce documentation and workload at the operation level and promote Management by Walking Around (MBWA). In ensuring a smooth transition of the payment procedure, Mr Ahmad has explained the new procedure with MC, the only service provider of the company. From thereon, all invoices from MC need to be forwarded to HQ Housekeeping Department for payment process. During this time, Mr Faris and Ms Rini have just been transferred to the department as managers and officers. Therefore, both of them have to get familiar with the new procedures introduced by Mr Ahmad.

While at the outlet, every outlet's hygiene and cleanliness performance and standard will be monitored by the housekeeping supervisor at each mall and store. The housekeeping supervisor will liaise with HQ Housekeeping Department if there are any arising matters with a service provider that could not be resolved at the operational level. Regarding the cleaning service performance, the HQ Housekeeping Department directed all Housekeeping supervisors to conduct the weekly audit with the service provider at each outlet. The results will be shared the following month, and each mall needs to rectify issues at their store if their audit result is unsatisfactory, below 80%. MC shall submit the delivery order of the items they ordered and delivered to the outlet for services and delivery. Monthly ordering and delivery for hygiene and consumable items will follow the quantity stated in the agreement. The housekeeping Supervisor is no longer need to do monthly order for hygiene items such as tissue, garbage bag, floor mat, air freshener, foam soap and chemicals. Previously, each Housekeeping Supervisor at the NEXTRA outlet is required to do monthly ordering on their own.

In 2016, NEXTRA signed a Tripartite Agreement with their sister company, NCM and their long-time cleaning service provider, MC. In the Tripartite Agreement, NEXTRA is expected to receive a good standard of cleaning services and monitor by NCM based on the agreed costs and terms and conditions. Previously, NEXTRA received services directly from cleaning contractors, either MC or NCM. Still, NCM shall act as Project Manager, and NEXTRA does not communicate directly with the service provider after the agreement. NEXTRA will have to report and discuss any issues about cleaning services with the Project Manager, including billing and invoicing of services. NCM will receive a commission of 8% from the cost charged by the service provider to NEXTRA. Therefore, NEXTRA is expecting its project manager's effectiveness in managing the cleaning services at all times.

This tripartite agreement is aimed to reduce the burden of NEXTRA and the Housekeeping Department in monitoring their contractor since NEXTRA already have outlets all around Malaysia. HQ Housekeeping Department faces difficulties in managing their malls and stores nationwide due to a lack of staff. NCM was established in Malaysia in 2012; therefore, the company may not have solid and extensive knowledge and experience in retail cleaning services. Unlike MC, it has worked with NEXTRA since 2000, which means they have been supporting NEXTRA retail business for 18 years now. The relationship between NEXTRA and MC were undeniably strong, and there is no doubt that these two companies require support from each other to grow in Malaysia.

In the same year, business was not going so well for NEXTRA when the government imposed GST and minimum wages for every employee at RM1,000.00. Due to the enforcement,

NEXTRA had forced to cut down their operational expenses, including cleaning services. As for Housekeeping Department, they had to reduce 100pax of manpower at the NEXTRA outlet to ensure their costs did not exceed their yearly budget. Through this exercise, the cost was reduced by almost 2.6% as compared to last year. Later in 2017, when the government implemented the levy charges on employers, MC transferred the cost of manpower to NCM, and NCM will charge NEXTRA for the levy charges. Although there was no proper discussion about this cost, NEXTRA had to face an increment in manpower cost and decided to reduce another 77 pax of manpower at their outlet.

The company

NEXTRA had an extended history with their current cleaning service provider since they started their occupational in Malaysia in the 1980s. They aim to serve and give the best experience to their customers throughout their shopping experience. NEXTRA is known for its philosophy, "To serve the Customer First". In NEXTRA, they are always acquainted with these three keywords:' peace', 'people' and 'community' and how important these three words are in building and creating the soul and reputation of the retail industry and must always be considered in any expansion they involve in. NEXTRA business is known as a person-to-person business, and its existence is deeply entwined with people in the regional neighbourhood and societies they serve. NEXTRA act as a contributing member of the local community, and these credits would remain the same wherever they do business all around the nation.

In NEXTRA Co. (M) Bhd, the departments are divided into different divisions, which are the Corporate Management Division, Corporate Planning Division, Mall Business Division and Retail General Merchandise Store (GMS) Business. The Mall Business manage total NEXTRA Mall businesses include tenant, leasing, and building management. Unlike Retail (GMS) Business, this division manages general merchandise stores, also known as the departmental stores that provide day-to-day products to the customers.

Under the Mall Business Division, four departments are the Development & Construction Department, Mall Leasing & Marketing Department, Mall Operation & Credit Control Department, and Asset & Facility Management. The Asset & Facility Management Department consists of Facility Department, Security Department, Safety Department, and Housekeeping Department. Even though the Housekeeping Department is allocated under Mall Business Division, the department also need to monitor the cleaning services and performance at departmental stores in the NEXTRA outlet.

Though 2015 and 2016 had been challenging years for most retailers, NEXTRA had increases in sales for the entire company from the year 2012 until 2016, with more than 1 new outlet opened for business each year, referring to NEXTRA Co. (M) Bhd. 2016 Annual Report. However, with the growing total sales for the company, NEXTRA still struggles in Malaysia financial recession when operational costs are also increased, leading to declining profitability. Due to this crisis, non-profit departments are usually being embattled to reduce their operating cost each year. Operational costs also have enlarged since there is a rise in the cost of most raw materials after GST implementation in 2015.

In 2017, NEXTRA had few changes at the top level when a new Managing Director (MD) is appointed, Mr Asahi from Japan, replacing the former MD, Ms Zarin. With the recent appointment of MD, a new direction has been introduced, namely "Back to Basic". It is a new direction for the whole company to increase productivity, improve pro-activeness, and increase monitoring to control their expenses and budget. The cost centre department is one of the most affected since the department is a non-profit department and contribute to high costs, including the Housekeeping Department. At the end of the year 2016, the department has set up a new budget for 2017, and it appears that the Housekeeping Department has come out with a budget reduction of 5.44% against last year for all NEXTRA Store outlets in Malaysia.

The issues: Documentation in the flow of requisition and proposal (R&P)

After the announcement by Mr Asahi about the need to recheck and monitor every department expenses to ensure the department complies with the proper practice in managing business and costs. The housekeeping department has been receiving a visit from IA's personnel, Ms Rina. Since the direction is to check on the department's expenses, IA requested Ms Rini to prepare a set of R&P copies from 2015 to 2017.

Starting from the year 2015, the Housekeeping Department has been responsible for preparing a centralized monthly payment voucher for the entire company cleaning services charge(s). Every department must prepare the R&P and signed by an authorised person before any outsource work can be done at a NEXTRA outlet. Then, since the amount charged for cleaning services is considerable, the R&P required approval from the Managing Director's office. Once the cleaning services company fulfils the cleaning service(s), the department will receive an invoice(s) from the supplier and be processed further for payment. This practice continued after signing the Tripartite Agreement between the three parties.

After the signing of the Tripartite Agreement between the three parties, the Housekeeping department is still required to prepare the R&P and approval before payment can be made by the Finance department. During the audit, the auditor has checked the date of R&P approval and the Tripartite Agreement. It is written in the document that they received approval for R&P from MD in March 2016, but the agreement was signed by the department's GM in February 2016. Supposedly, they can only sign the agreement with NCM and MC once the budget is approved, but the documentation shows otherwise.

Mr Faris explained to IA, and the GM has received a verbal agreement from the MD to sign the Tripartite Agreement with details of total cleaning service costs. However, oral agreement upon signing the R&P is not acceptable since top management could shift as what has happened in recent years. After discovering the wrong procedure, Ms Rini sincerely apologized to her manager because she prepared the R&P and did not know the actual SOP for R&P and the agreement signing process. They discussed the countermeasure to avoid the same mistake from happening again in the future.

This practice was not aligned with the company R&P policy. As a result, the agreement and R&P in the year 2016 did not comply with the Company's Finance policy, and it will be included in the audit findings. In addition, it requires countermeasure and improvement from HQ Housekeeping Department to avoid the same mistake from happening again in the future.

Criticism and compliance

Criticism by other departments towards the Housekeeping department's performance in managing and monitoring cleaning service contractors has had an impact on Ms Rini's annual KPI evaluation. Although she is new in the department, it is still her responsibility in ensuring cleaning service contractors deliver work as per NEXTRA's standards and expectations. Ms Rini remembered in one interview, one of the panel mentioned to her when she was defensive about the downgraded performance of the cleaning service provider at NEXTRA outlets. The panel said to Ms Rini, "Although our MD's policy is 'Back to Basic' it does not mean that we should lower our cleaning services standard although you managed to reduce the cost by thousands of Ringgit every month. Condition at mall and store is now getting worse with the reduction of cleaner manpower at all outlet." There are still lots of areas that need improvement in the department.

After the changing of management in the division and Mr Kamal joined the division, the payment process is more scrutinised in accordance with the Standard Operating Procedures (SOP). It requires relevant documentation as proof of work done before his approval. Mr Kamal complained that MC has shown that they have few documentation issues, and there were lots of work done without any consent from the outlet. Therefore, he refused to approve some of the invoices submitted to him. In addition, the way the HQ Housekeeping Department do the checking and monitoring of payment is questioned by Mr Kamal. Mr Kamal requested HQ Housekeeping Department to work closely together with the Housekeeping Supervisor at the NEXTRA outlet to ensure any misconduct by the service provider can be reported efficiently.

Due to the arising matter raised by Mr Kamal, Mr Faris requested Ms Rini to prepare a report based on their weekly visit at the NEXTRA outlet. Compilation of comments and issues by the personnel at the operation level should be compiled and recorded to keep track of the improvement on every matter that arises during the visits. Mr Faris also voiced out his concern about MC's working style with NEXTRA. He felt that it had been continued from the previous year that there is a lack of transparency between NEXTRA and MC.

After she visited the selected outlet during the week, Ms Rini compiled all the complaints she received from the selected outlets as follows;

1. Late delivery of hygiene and consumable items; tissue, garbage bag, foam soap, air freshener, and floor mat. These items are all contractual items; therefore, there should be no delay in delivery since they receive the same quantity of hygiene and consumable items every month.
2. Cleaner attitude problems. Due to lack of training or lack of communication skills among foreign workers from Bangladesh, Nepal, Myanmar, and Pakistan, our local staff have problems communicating and giving direction to them.
3. Few outlets complained that supplier allocated old and unused machineries at their outlet. But, on the other

hand, supplier machines like IMEC took a long time to collect the machines and consumed spaces in their backroom.
4. Poor quality of floor mat that contribute to hazard and accident to customers. One incident happened in NEXTRA Mall Bukit Indah where a customer slipped on the floor due to the poor quality of the floor mat provided by the service provider.
5. No signage during cleaning work in progress.
6. Working permit issue. As per agreed, the supplier shall provide staff (cleaner) with a valid passport and working permit all the time they are working in NEXTRA premises. The latest issue arose at the operational level within the month. Few foreign workers could not present their valid working permits due to the late renewal process and newcomers into Malaysia.
7. A crowded and busy outlet like NEXTRA Southern City and NEXTRA Store in the Central complained that service provider allocated senior and non-performer staffs at their outlet with a high number of customers daily.
8. Late response by cleaner supervisor at NEXTRA outlet.

In accordance with Clause 4.2 of the agreement, for any unsatisfied performance, NEXTRA has the right to issue a reminder letter or impose a penalty or terminate the agreement. Based on the clause in the agreement, Ms Rina has further inquiry regarding the responsibilities of the Housekeeping department. After she did checking on monthly service payments, the DOs are not included as the supporting document. The listed issues are submitted to MC and NCM offices for their attention and immediate action.

Ms Rini has performed further investigation throughout the week to get more information about the overall complaints. She discovered that their concerns towards the transparency of NCM and MC are genuinely questionable. She has gathered several delivery order documents and managed to prove that MC has been supplying NEXTRA with different types of chemicals and less quantity of chemicals and machineries than per agreed. Before forwarding all the documents to her manager, she realized that NCM has failed to ensure MC's efficiency, honesty, and productivity. She detected issues in a particular part of the cleaning services and has listed them in an email to Mr Faris. The email to Mr Faris is as follows;

"Dear Mr Faris,

After a week of reviewing and analysing the documents given by NCM. Also, I cross-checked it with other documents and reflet to my compilation of complaints from my recent visits to some of the outlets. The following is my findings;

MC (the Service Provider):

1. Lack of transparency in doing business with NEXTRA
    a. Unable to give proper documentation as proof of services performed.
2. On a monthly basis, the items delivered to the NEXTRA outlet did not comply with the list of items agreed in the tripartite agreement.
3. Some of the work was being done without any consent from the client (NEXTRA).

NCM (the Project Manager):

1. Failure in ensuring the efficiency and productivity of Service Provider
2. A discrepancy in the specification of machineries and types of chemicals delivered to NEXTRA outlets were identified
3. The service Provider changed the contract quantity without any consent from the client
4. The quotation and invoices issued by NCM were without a detailed breakdown
5. The invoice(s) were overbilled by NCM. This resulted in clients being overpaid for services that they did not receive. In addition, the issuance of credit note(s) due to the amount overbilled were late.

The findings that were discovered proved that discrepancy existed. These further support that our cleaning services provider did not honour the details of products and services in the Tripartite Agreement. Furthermore, NCM did not oversee and monitor the cleaning services received by the client is in accordance with the items agreed in the agreement.

Your kind attention on this matter is highly appreciated. Thank you.

Best regards,

Rini."

The finding of negligence and dishonesty of their supplier has urged the team to find ways to prove the wrongdoings to ensure there will be a sum of payback for the services they did not obtain at total NEXTRA outlets. When a person or a company in business with a deal breaches a legal obligation or falls short of fulfilling an obligation as stated in the agreement term, it is considered negligence. In addition, in some cases, a person or company management is considered criminally negligent.

Since Mr Faris is still on holiday, Ms Rini went to see their AGM to communicate about the findings that she discovered and the issues they are facing. "Sir, my findings were documented in this file. I compile these findings through my visit to a few outlets. I made comparisons on products stipulated in the agreement and products supplied to the outlet. It seems that discrepancy exists. These are the proof that some outlets have been receiving quantity and types of chemical not as agreed in the agreement."

"Previously, how did we manage the documents for payment, and why did we only realise and detect this problem now?" asked Mr Kamal after he glanced through the issues reported by his staff. "Previously, I did not receive some of these documents. All documents are submitted by MC through NCM. Since all our invoices came from NCM, we need our operation personnel to acknowledge that the items were delivered to their outlet." Ms Rini tried to convince Mr Kamal that the Project Manager has not carried out their responsibilities towards their primary client. Due to the discrepancy issue tabled by Ms Rini, En Kamal urged a meeting with the service provider.

Foreign workers permits

In the afternoon, before Ms Rini went out for lunch, she received a phone call from the receptionist saying few workers wanted to see her in the office lobby. It is unusual for her to receive any visit from the foreign worker because she is not in charge of the foreign worker directly. When she arrived at the lobby, she saw two Bangladeshi workers waiting for her. She recognized one of the workers; he is one of the cleaner supervisors from the NEXTRA outlet in Central Township. They were not wearing uniforms means they are not currently in working hours. After she meets with the service provider's employees, she understands that a few foreign workers are in the process of renewing their working permits with the Immigration Department. Therefore, they were not allowed to enter and work at the NEXTRA outlet. Ms Sara was overwhelmed, the discrepancy issues were still in progress, and now she is facing another issue of the foreign workers.

Referring to the tripartite agreement, it clearly stated that every foreign worker must have a valid passport and working permit to work with us. There should be no excuse for the supplier in fulfilling the requirement since they have worked for NEXTRA for a number of years. In Clause 8.2 (d) in the Tripartite Agreement, abide by all laws about the employment of foreign workers, if applicable. As such, the Service Provider shall, where applicable, submit copies of the relevant documents, including but not limited to the following documents to the client for inspection and record purposes:

i. Work permits;
ii. Valid International Passports;
iii. Health Examination Reports; and
iv. Criminal Records, if any.

Supposedly, the Project Manager and Service Provider shall ensure that all foreign workers must have a valid passport and working permit. Now that both NCM and MC failed to resolve issues involving their employees, is it possible to take legal action to improve this matter in the near future? When it is related to law and authority, it could also jeopardise NEXTRA image and brand if the issue is not being handled very well.

Case questions

1. What are the problems that were faced by Housekeeping Department, NEXTRA Co. (M) Bhd.? How would these problems impact NEXTRA business?
2. What are the advantages and disadvantages of outsourcing in providing services to a company?
3. What are the recommendations that you would offer to Housekeeping Department to improve their current practice?
4. What is the role of Mr Kamal in dealing with issues faced by the Housekeeping Department in ensuring optimum level of service delivery and service quality that are offered to NEXTRA's customers?
5. In the internal audit process, the IA highlighted issues related to documentation and compliance to the Standards Operating Procedures. In your opinion, how the improvement towards the governance issues would improve the current problems that Housekeeping Department faces? Could you recommend some improvement to the corporate governance aspect practice in NEXTRA?

www.ingramcontent.com/pod-product-compliance
Lightning Source LLC
Chambersburg PA
CBHW030802180526
45163CB00003B/1136